# The Fundamentals of Product Design
## Richard Morris

ava |Academia
the environment of learning

An AVA Book

Published by AVA Publishing SA

Rue des Fontenailles 16
Case Postale
1000 Lausanne 6
Switzerland

Tel: +41 786 005 109
Email: enquiries@avabooks.ch

Distributed by Thames & Hudson (ex-North America)

181a High Holborn
London WC1V 7QX
United Kingdom

Tel: +44 20 7845 5000
Fax: +44 20 7845 5055
Email: sales@thameshudson.co.uk
www.thamesandhudson.com

Distributed in the USA and Canada by Ingram Publisher Services Inc.

1 Ingram Blvd.
La Vergne, TN 37086
USA

Tel: +1 866 400 5351
Fax: +1 800 838 1149
Email: customer.service@ingrampublisherservices.com

English Language Support Office

AVA Publishing (UK) Ltd.
Tel: +44 1903 204 455
Email: enquiries@avabooks.ch

ISBN 978-2-940373-17-8 and 2-940373-17-5

10 9 8 7 6 5 4 3 2 1

Design by David Shaw

Production by AVA Book Production Pte. Ltd., Singapore

Tel: +65 6334 8173
Fax: +65 6259 9830
Email: production@avabooks.com.sg

All reasonable attempts have been made to trace, clear and credit
the copyright holders of the images reproduced in this book.
However, if any credits have been inadvertently omitted, the publisher
will endeavour to incorporate amendments in future editions.

**Richard Morris**

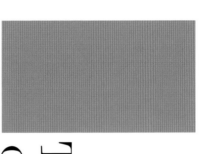

# The Fundamentals of Product Design

Academia
the environment of learning

# Table of contents

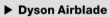

## ▶ Dyson Airblade

Dyson's hand dryer uses a small brushless motor, which runs at 100,000 revolutions per minute to force filtered air through two apertures, creating fast-moving sheets of air that 'scrape' water from wet hands. It's quick, hygienic and uses significantly less energy than traditional warm-air hand dryers.

Photograph: Dyson Ltd.

# Introduction

Humans have been designing products for hundreds of thousands of years: fashioning tools from wood and stone; building heat-retaining fireplaces for cooking; adorning their bodies with artefacts and ornaments and painting on walls using hollow-reed spray brushes. Animals, too, have learnt to design and many forms of mammal, insect and invertebrate are capable of designing and building beds and doorways, or fashioning poking and hunting implements. Product design might therefore be considered an inherent and inbuilt organic activity and might explain why the act of design is so intrinsically satisfying to so many people. Product design can offer a rewarding career; whether you are a 'superstar' designer working on a range of high-profile consumer products, or a part of a large team working on components that may never even be seen or noticed by the general public.

The challenge for today's designer, however, is the sheer complexity of our world; the rate of change that our society experiences and the breadth and depth of information available and required. Designers must gather, process and incorporate this information in an effective manner, even when it can seem confusing and overwhelming. Our competitive world places additional pressures on the designer in its demands for speed and accuracy: products must be created quickly with calls that they are 'right first time'. So whilst it can be a rewarding career, it does not automatically follow that product design is easy.

To help the designer, there is a growing body of research into design tools and methods. However, this too can lead to additional confusion. Which tools should a designer use and which methods should they follow? Design means different things to different people and few people would say there is one right way to design, or one right set of tools. For some, design is all about creativity and creation. For others, it's a skill or an art. To others still, it might be all about process. Whilst this makes design a rich subject to study and practice, it can make it difficult to write a book with definitions and content that will please everyone.

Product design, in particular, covers an enormous number of topics with a knowledge requirement that is never ending, which again makes it a fascinating career choice, but a challenge for any design writer trying to squeeze a coherent body of work into one book. However, this book does provide an overview of information from a range of different perspectives

**▲ Copper Shade Pendant by Tom Dixon**

This lamp shade is made from polycarbonate that has been blown into a spherical, open-mouthed mould to create the bubble-shaped design.

Photograph: Tom Dixon

## A multifaceted approach

*The Fundamentals of Product Design* provides a little of all of these perspectives. It highlights a range of design issues, looking, for example, at the technical knowledge required or the skills that can be needed. In so doing, it aims to provide an integrated and cohesive view of the design process that designers can sometimes find hard to grasp or can lose sight of. In this way, the book provides a framework for understanding the fundamentals of product design, with pointers to more advanced thinking where designers might strive to become more proficient.

This book does not have all the answers, but its objective is to help you develop your own design style and ideas. In so doing it aims to help everybody, since it is through the work of designers that we can all enjoy a better world.

# How to use this book

*The Fundamentals of Product Design* can be read in its entirety to gain an insight into the scope and context of product design. It can also be read with equal value as a reference book, dipping into sections and pages as you work through a real design problem. The information provided may direct you towards areas that you need to think about, help you understand issues, or point you towards sources of further information.

Another way to read the book is to select pages at random. Some of the book's case studies and examples feature a number of the world's most famous and experienced designers, while others are by younger and less famous designers. Some of the products are expensive and luxurious, whilst others are everyday consumables. None of the designs for these products will have been achieved without some effort (and most likely some anxiety on the designer's part) and knowing this can be helpful when you face your own design problems. Be inspired, therefore, by the work on display and by the challenges and achievements of good design.

# Tom Dixon

**Biography**
Tom Dixon describes himself as 'a self-educated maverick whose only qualification is a one-day course in plastic bumper repair'. His early life saw him experience a variety of different cultures and his early creative works are marked by a personal interest in welding, which allowed him to create structures quickly from scrap (one of which led to his collaboration with Italian furniture company Cappellini and the realisation of the celebrated 'S' chair).

Dixon prefers to be considered an industrialist, yet he is regarded as a highly creative designer by most and has many product awards to his name. He has also been scathing towards British manufacturing and design bodies for not supporting British design and innovation sufficiently. He attempted to resolve this by setting up his own British company, Eurolounge.

**Habitat**
Dixon's experience with both Cappellini and Eurolounge represented a journey away from the realm of a jobbing industrialist creator to that of a more business-savvy designer. This direction went a step further when he accepted the role of Head of Design in the UK for international home furnishing retailer Habitat.

Placing a maverick into a mainstream, corporate, retail-driven business was a risky strategy for both Habitat and Dixon. Dixon, however, was pleased to learn more about mass production, manufacturing and costing and to have access to a worldwide basket of design possibilities. In fact, he has described his decision to learn more about developing commercial products as a state of 'growing up'.

**Blow Light** (facing page),
**Slab Chair** (this page, top)
and **Fresh Fat Easy Chair**
(this page, bottom) **all by
Tom Dixon**
Photographs: Tom Dixon

In return he gave Habitat a highly successful makeover. Among his initiatives were the reintroduction of design classics and the fostering of new design talent. Dixon later became Habitat's Creative Director and was awarded an OBE for his services to design.

Dixon has not compromised his individuality in order to be commercially successful. He continues to be innovative, creative and controversial, yet can design successfully for both the high end and the mainstream markets. He has a continuing thirst for knowledge too: ask about his current work, and he talks not just about design, ideas and creation, but about his interest in engineering, marketing, manufacturing processes and digital production.

## Case studies
Commercial projects from contemporary product designers bring the principles under discussion alive.

## Biographies
Each case study is introduced by a short biography of the product designer featured.

## Product information
Contains detailed and contextual information about products and practices referenced in the body text.

## Captions
Supply contextual information about the images and reference key concepts discussed in the body copy.

## Body text
The body text outlines the fundamental principles of product design.

## Images
Photographs and illustrations from an array of professional practices bring the text to life.

# Chapter 1

The Fundamentals of Product Design

# Product ideas

I have tried to develop my own approach to design and my own idea of what design is or, more interestingly, what it could be. My main interest is in making new and different stuff by using the knowledge I collect as a hobby and mainly about technology and how we relate to it.
**Mathias Bengtsson, Bengtsson Design Ltd.**

**Approximately two million patent applications are made every year. Many of these are generated by companies recognising that new products are the key to economic survival. It is just one example of the new, creative industrial revolution. These applications, however, are just the tip of a global ideas iceberg and exclude even more ideas that never get to the patent stage. But just where do these ideas keep coming from? This chapter explores two routes to the creation of new product ideas.**

◄ **MT3 Rocking Chair by Ron Arad for Driade**

# Imagination

The ability to come up with new product ideas need not be restricted to just a few creative people or talented designers – *everybody* has an imagination. A designer is, however, able to generate new ideas time and time again for any number of different projects and this is one of the features that distinguishes a 'professional' designer from a casual inventor. This section looks at some of the ways that professional designers are able to systematically produce such great product ideas through the power of imagination.

### Taking a different view

If people simply copied the work of others, then nothing new would ever emerge. Even just thinking in the same way would result in products that were broadly similar. Yet thinking against the grain does not necessarily come easily and there is a natural herd-like instinct to follow the crowd. It's safer, and there may be a presumption that everyone else might be right or that if things have always been done that way, then that must be the best way of doing it.

Designers rarely accept this, which is why good design often looks fresh and exciting. Look with an open mind at life around you – not just at products, but also at their everyday details. Accept that everything you know might be wrong, and that everything other people do, say or know might also be wrong. This does not mean being contrary or argumentative; but it does mean being prepared to question everything, being able to hold a different view and being able to voice an alternative opinion.

### Gaining new experiences

It can be difficult to take a different view if the life you lead is closeted or routine. Imagine growing up and living within an enclosed room where everything inside was blue. If you were asked to design something new, your products would inevitably be blue. Similarly, if you routinely follow the same customs and habits, hold the same thoughts, follow the same routes or see the same sights, then your capacity to learn about, compare and contrast ideas becomes equally limited. In fact, a set pattern of thinking can actually create rigid thought processes that restrict our ability to be creative.

New experiences might take the form of large-scale change, such as travelling or living in a new country, but might equally mean just reading a different newspaper, talking to someone new or sitting on a different seat on the train. Great designers are always ready to tackle new challenges, work with new people and try new things.

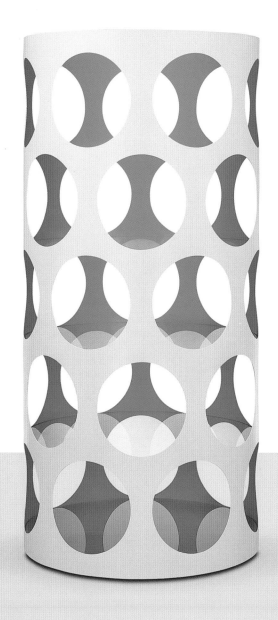

### ▲ Wood Chair by Marc Newson

Newson's Wood Chair is a refinement of his earlier Embryo Chair, made simpler with a more abstract double 'hourglass' curve. It was originally made as an exhibition piece, but was later taken up as a production piece and manufactured by Italian design company Cappellini.

Photograph:
Marc Newson Ltd.

### ◀ Bubble Storage Unit by Aziz Sariyer

Sariyer's aluminium Bubble Storage Unit is lacquered on the outside and painted on the inside with phosphoric primary colours. It has four clear glass shelves, making a practical product, but at nearly two metres tall it offers a different perspective by providing shelving that also has a standalone, sculptural quality.

Imagination ▼ Case study: Wayne Hemingway

▶ **Massive Infection by Pieke Bergmans**

Young Dutch designer Pieke Bergmans's favourite design methods include subverting existing production processes to create new forms and functions, which she then describes in terms of virus or infection. Bergmans claims that her designs stem from an unstoppable curiosity.

## Exploration and playing

Exploration is another way of achieving new experiences and ideas. Some of the world's best innovations have come not from experts but from ordinary people who were trying to discover or better understand something. Alexander Graham Bell, for example, invented the telephone – but he was not an engineer. In fact, the great inventor Thomas Edison said that if Bell had known more about electricity, he would never have invented the telephone.

The Internet makes a whole world of knowledge accessible within seconds, and may have a role to play in enabling people to learn and explore further; but exploration might also mean asking 'what if' or 'how can' questions, and talking to others. Physical exploration can be equally illuminating; finding and working with materials, shapes, patterns, taking things apart to see how they work, or building mock-ups and models are all valid options. This sort of research does not have to be precise, or even purposeful, but may simply be a means to producing a library of new thoughts and knowledge.

Playing can have an important role in exploration. Adults have a greater capacity for abstraction and our models of learning move further towards didactic and instructional ones as we grow older. This is fine for some subjects, but not for others – and can prove to be unrealistic and tiresome for long periods of exploration and learning. Designers, therefore, have no qualms in reverting to a play mode in order to assist their creative thinking, in much the same way that young children learn.

It can also be more illuminating to experiment, explore, mimic or make something with no purpose other than to think in a purely abstract way; or in trying to apply knowledge solely according to rules and logic. Having fun through play also reduces stress and being more relaxed can help the thinking process. Many design-focused organisations recognise this too, and may have spaces for staff to play, or may encourage playful activities.

## Subversion

It is easy to think that there is always one, or a best or right answer to a problem. It is arguable that our rational approach to life and upbringing trains us to be logical and analytical and hence to seek these unique solutions. Designers, however, approach a problem knowing that there is always more than one answer to be found. This approach is one of the core skills of a designer; that lends itself not just to design but to an approach to life in general.

One way to implement this philosophy is to explore as many workable ideas as possible. Most designers use sketchbooks to capture ideas in simple forms whilst they are working or on the move. To come up with new ideas might sometimes mean breaking the rules – such as the rules of nature, or society, or social etiquette. This activity can have a subversive quality to it, but it can also lead to profound new thinking and design.

I roamed the countryside searching for answers to things I did not understand.
**Leonardo da Vinci**

### Adaptation

It's often human nature to think that the best solution must be radical and new, but in fact improvements can be quite minor and subtle. This doesn't mean designers should aim to release boring work: quite profound effects can be achieved simply by adapting existing designs in simple ways, such as changing scales, altering features or redefining attributes.

Designers look not just at existing products but also at the work of other designers. This does not mean copying the work of others, but does mean learning from the way that they work and think. What are other designers working on? What are they thinking? How did they get to where they are? Exhibitions, design magazines, networks and forums are some of the ways that this can be done easily and effectively.

### Lessons from nature

The flora, fauna and patterns of the world around us have been evolving over millions of years, so there are great lessons and ideas that can be learnt from nature. How do owls fly silently? What are fractals? Why don't fish in swarms bump into one another? The term bionics, amongst others, is used to describe the application of nature's biological methods and systems to the fields of engineering and design. There are many examples, such as the echo location of bats which is mimicked in sonar or medical scanning; or the small plant burrs that attach themselves to the fur or clothing of passing animals or people, which inspired the creation of Velcro.

### Reflection

Our modern lifestyles incorporate immense time pressures that lead us to act quickly, eat quickly, pack the day with activities and find an idea quickly. This busyness can, in itself, stop us having the time to experiment, to learn or play and can sometimes cut down our opportunities for imaginative thought; but it can also stop the mental process of thinking about and reflecting on life all around us.

Most people will recollect an inspired thought that came during moments of tranquillity and relaxation, perhaps when in the bath, in bed, in the bar, or waiting for a bus with nothing else to do. Often, therefore, reflection means just taking some time out to rest in order to be able to think, freewheel, daydream, reflect and let your imagination work. Even sleeping itself can refresh the brain's synapses, enabling new thoughts to evolve.

Whilst this might seem relatively straightforward, it can be counter-intuitive and it often takes determination to actually stop and take a reflective break amid the frenzy of life. There are, however, many activities that will stimulate reflective practice including meditation, yoga, taking a regular walk, or carrying a digital camera or notebook around in order to encourage and capture thoughtful or reflective moments.

### ◀ Mezzadro Stool by Castiglioni

The Mezzadro Stool is an aluminium tractor seat attached to a chrome-plated steel stem with a beech footrest. It is an example of a 'ready-made', drawing on everyday objects to make design pieces. The adaptation of a tractor seat has been lauded for its expressive strength, starting as an exhibition piece before being taken up for production by Zanotta.

### ▶ not a lamp by David Graas

not a lamp incorporates a silhouette of a light in the lamp's shade. It's this silhouette that then glows rather than the space around it, offering a subtle but unusual perspective. The shade is assembled in a parody of flat-pack furniture (as shown in the line diagram, far right).

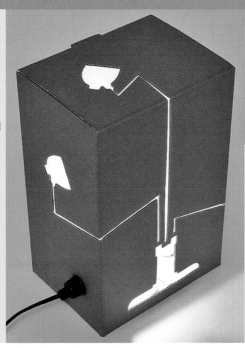

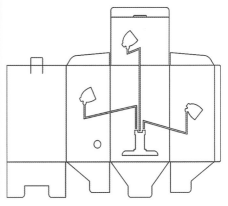

Imagination ▼ Case study: Wayne Hemingway

## ▶ Porsche Design Multihammer (P'7911)

Ferdinand Porsche founded the Porsche Design Group and although it is separate to the Porsche car company, it is part of the same manufacturing group. This subtle distinction is likely to be rendered immaterial to most consumers since the design group has applied many affordances of Porsche cars to their other design projects. The Metabo Multihammer, for example, has a carbon fibre/aluminium body that makes it lighter and sleeker, and a unique ergonomic shape.

## Working with materials

Less experienced designers can sometimes consider materials far too late in the design process, often as something that needs to be chosen in order to finish or house the product. This might simply be a choice between metal and plastic, or between a range of primary plastics such as ABS or polypropylene thermoplastics.

In fact, there are thousands and thousands of materials offering an incredible range of characteristics and performances that a designer can explore at the front end of the design process just to stimulate ideas. Many companies house a library or selection of materials for this purpose. Exploration might be through a tactile or visual appearance; brushed aluminium, for example, has a smooth, satisfying grain but is marked easily with greasy fingers. Exploration might also be through function and performance.

The vast range of emerging materials makes exploration even more relevant. Developments in nano technology, composites, bio-composites, gels, foams and treatments offer designers incredible new opportunities. For example, d3o, is a soft material engineered with intelligent molecules that 'flow' with you as you move, but lock together when hit hard to form a solid object (see pages 122–123). Terfenol™, for example, expands or contracts within a magnetic field and has found roles in innovative products from loudspeakers to mining props. Aerogel is a hazy blue sponge-like substance that is made from the same material as glass but is formed from 99.8% air, making it 1,000 times less dense. What product ideas might you fashion from these materials?

## Technology

'Technology' can be an elusive term to define precisely, but might broadly encompass the knowledge and application of tools, crafts and science that we use to shape the world. Hence although it would include common associations such as information technology or the advanced high technologies of the aerospace industries, it might equally include notions of systems, methods and in fact anything that brings about change. Like new materials, new technologies can therefore have the capacity to generate new product ideas on a massive scale.

The issues for designers is being able to access new technological developments since many will be confidential or lay hidden within company research labs with potential that remains unrealised. There is a further issue in understanding new techniques and technologies. Networking events, trade exhibitions, science magazines, technology transfer and patent sites and partnerships between designers and technologists might release new opportunities by helping to outline and explain technologies.

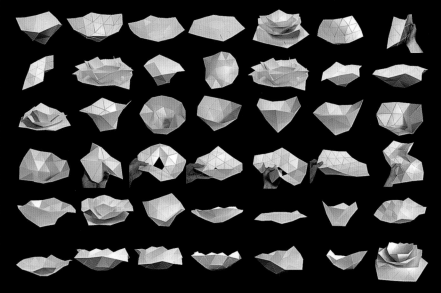

◄ **Crushed bowls by Julien de Smedt/ Maria Ljungsten for Muuto**

Julien de Smedt has applied the same principles of equilateral triangles used in the computer-aided design of architectural projects to the design of this range of bowls. The bowls are made of bone china and are unglazed and hand-polished on the outside and glazed on the inside. The bowls retail through Danish company Muuto.

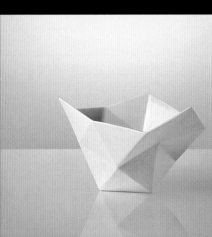

▶ **The WildCharge™ pad**

The WildCharge™ pad is an example of wire-free power transfer technology. Products with batteries that need recharging are placed on to the conductive surface and receive power no matter how they are orientated.

Photograph: WildCharge™ Inc.

### ▶ Segway by Dean Kamen

Despite having just two wheels, Segway transporters are able to self-balance and remain upright, providing a novel way of steering and travelling. This is achieved through the development of 'dynamic stabilisation' technology revolving around five micro machined gyroscopic sensors. These solid-state (silicon) devices utilise the Coriolis effect to determine the angular turning rate, which provides feedback information to the motors allowing corrections to be made and keeping the device upright.

Photographs: segway.com

Imagination ▼ Case study: Wayne Hemingway

## New ways and making links

Doing things differently can be thought-provoking. Try pulling a wheelbarrow instead of pushing it, lacing your shoes in a new way, reading a newspaper back to front, eating breakfast at night and dinner in the morning, or using tea leaves instead of tea bags. This is similar to the process of thinking differently and experimenting, but is less general and aimed at specific products and artefacts. The insights that come from these activities can spark new insights, trains of thought and ideas.

One of the most powerful of creative techniques is to form links between previously unassimilated areas. An adult might never consider it possible to combine a car and a washing machine to make a washing machine car, but a small child has no problem in doing this or in making any other number of seemingly illogical connections. But why not have a small washing machine in the car? There is water, heat and motion for tumbling and drying. Sometimes the ideas go nowhere, but occasionally new breakthroughs will occur.

Some designers have become famous for the ideas they have pioneered or excelled in. Raymond Loewy (considered by many to be an elder father of industrial design), for example, made much of new streamlining technology and applied this to products and equipment. Similarly, Dieter Rams's attempts to link timelessness with products produces trademark sleek and minimalist products that have an enduring, rather than trend-led, quality.

Over a period of time, the links formed by collections of designers create a style or a genre. Consider, for example, the ideological or practised ideas behind the Arts and Crafts movement, the art nouveau aesthetic, a modern company such as Sony, or the style of design collectives such as Droog.

## Industrial design

Both 'product design' and 'industrial design' are terms that have evolved over time. As a consequence, they mean different (and sometimes conflicting) things to different people. Broadly speaking, product design might be concerned with the efficient and effective generation and development of ideas through a process that leads to new products; whilst industrial design might be concerned with the aspect of that process that brings the sort of artistic form and usability usually associated with craft design to that of mass produced goods. Raymond Loewy's industrial designs have included the Shell logo, the Greyhound bus and S1 train and some of the earliest cars and refrigerators. These products are widely held to have impacted upon the shape of American culture. Dieter Rams was an advocate of the 'less is more' philosophy associated with Ludwig Mies van der Rohe which has influenced a wide range of European culture and design.

### ▶ Glass Tap by Arnout Visser for Droog

Much of Visser's work draws on his reflections upon physical or mechanical laws and on traditions of form and function. The resulting product often incorporates subtle humour or design twists, as is evident in Visser's Glass Tap.

Photograph:
Erik Jan Kwakkel

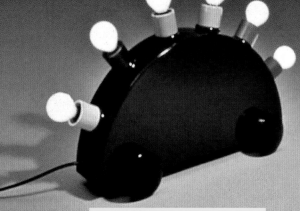

▲ **Super by Martine Bedin for Memphis**
Photograph: Aldo Ballo,
Guido Cegani, Peter Olgivie
www.memphis-milano.com

◄ **First by Michele De Lucchi for Memphis**
Photograph: Studio Azzurro,
Mitumasa Fujituka
www.memphis-milano.com

The Memphis group was a collective of Italian designers and architects that evolved from a meeting set up by designer Ettore Sottsass in the 1980s to challenge the then current status of design. The group contested the notion that good design revolved around slick, black, humourless and conformist products, and released a series of works that explored shapes, colours, textures and patterns.

The Super lamp was made from painted and lacquered metal and the First chair was designed from enamelled wood and metal.

Imagination ▼ Case study: Wayne Hemingway

### ▼ Moroso Misfits by Ron Arad

The idea of putting together a modular seating system with ill-matching shapes might never be a consideration for most designers and, if it were, it might then challenge natural sensibilities and be quickly and easily rejected. Yet Ron Arad's working of lines, curves and spaces produces a seat with a satisfying array of undulating movements.

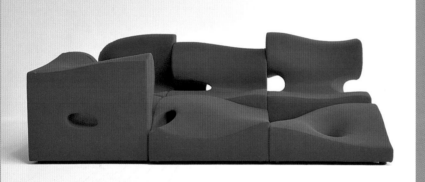

**◀ MT3 Rocking Chair by Ron Arad**
A rotationally moulded polyethylene rocking chair created for Driade by Ron Arad.

## Brainstorming techniques

Brainstorming is a group creativity technique designed to generate a large number of ideas in response to a problem. The method was first popularised in the late 1930s by advertising executive Alex Faickney Osborn. Sometimes the brainstorming principle is to remove prejudices, such as using the quick firing speed of ideas and images, as with **Pecha Kucha**. Edward de Bono's **Six Thinking Hats technique** involves adopting six different viewpoints in an effort to see a problem from a number of angles. **Brain writing 635** allows participants to take on elements of other people's ideas in a relatively 'blind' fashion. Morphological analysis is a linking together of all possible product attributes in an entirely random manner with the aim of producing interesting and previously unsought combinations.

## Creative techniques

Making new links between concepts is a powerful driver of creativity, but there are many other techniques that inspire creativity. These might be classified as techniques that prepare people to be more creative and imaginative, more receptive to ideas, and less rational and judgemental. These techniques have much in common with the activities that we have already looked at in earlier pages, but are more structured, and intense 'tools' to be applied as and when needed.

The best-known tool is that of brainstorming: encouraging people to generate ideas in a rapid, open and free group session. Its popularity is probably in direct proportion to its simplicity, but in reality it is a technique that is often poorly set up and run with insignificant results. Six Thinking Hats, Pecha Kucha, snowballing, morphological analysis, mind-mapping and Brain Writing 635 are among the many tools that may be worth investigating.

### ▶ Teletruck by JCB

The teletruck is a hybrid vehicle that incorporates a telescopic boom instead of standard lifting platform. It combines the strength and ruggedness of a digger with the flexibility of a forklift.

### ▶ Hedge Trimmer by Graham Wilson for Garden Groom

Traditional electric hedge trimmers have exposed blades that can cut through wires and leave a trail of debris that needs later collection. The Garden Groom has a concealed blade, which is not only safer but simultaneously shreds and collects debris. Despite this, all the garden tool producers that Wilson initially approached rejected the concept. Wilson therefore invested considerable money and risk in developing the product through to completion.

Photograph:
Garden Groom Ltd.

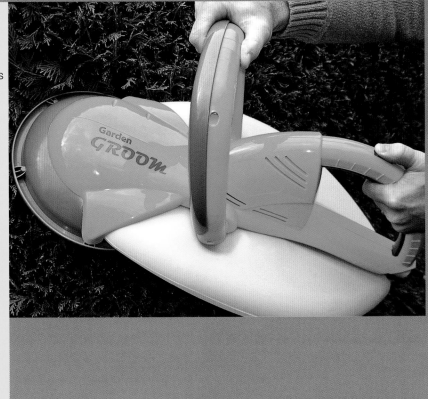

### ▼ boynq® Vase USB Speaker

The 5v and 100 and 500mA of power in the universal serial bus (USB) was originally intended to allow computer peripherals to be attached through a standardised connection without requiring a computer reboot. There are now around two billion USB devices in the world including boynq® Vase Speakers, which are powered through the USB port and include an 'acoustic' lens to simulate surround sound.

Photograph: boynq®

### Seizing opportunities

Generating ideas is one thing, but being able to recognise a new idea is something completely different. It is said that as many as 18 people may have had the opportunity to 'discover' antibiotics, but it was the recognition of the benefits of penicillin that lays this discovery firmly at the door of Alexander Fleming. Similarly, neither the inventor nor the original customer for the first electric light saw a market beyond their original brief. After all, gas and candles did the job!

Related to this is the notion of 'serendipity', which is a term that describes making a discovery whilst looking at something else that is completely unrelated. For example, in 1945 American engineer Percy Spencer noticed, whilst working on ways to mass-produce magnetrons needed for wartime radar systems, a gooey mass in his pocket. He realised that heat from the magnetron must have melted a bar of chocolate that was there. Many people may simply have ignored this phenomenon, but Spencer repeated the experiment with corn and eggs. His discovery led to Raytheon's (Spencer's employer) production of the world's first microwave cooker.

If generating ideas is one thing and recognising them another, then having the fortitude to work with them is something else again. Sometimes this can be easy. An obviously good idea can be exciting and motivating in itself. James Dyson was sufficiently confident of his dual cyclone technology that he was prepared to risk vast sums of money and time in the development of his new vacuum cleaner concept. But what if he had been wrong, or less certain of his ideas? The penalties for failure can be severe and it can be more comfortable to stick to the known. Designers must therefore have the courage to try new and uncertain ideas, even if the concepts are not clearly beneficial and there is a daunting risk of ridicule and failure.

# Wayne Hemingway

### Biography

Wayne Hemingway achieved initial success with his partner Geraldine through their bespoke fashion designs, which were sold from a stall in London's Camden Market; an enterprise that ultimately led to the launch of the Red or Dead fashion label. The label was lauded for its streetwise style and its willingness to challenge both the established fashion industry and the media on frequent occasions. Selling the business for multiple millions might have been a cue for retirement, but Hemingway subsequently engaged with a number of architectural and housing projects, challenging established thinking and winning numerous awards and design contracts in the process. His canon of work includes products such as digital radios and ceramic tiles and his clients include Sky Plus (Sky+), Wanadoo, British Ceramic Tile (BCT), Boddingtons, Sony, Royal Mail and the Caravan Club.

### The Shackup, HD Roadrunner and Butt Butt

A recent Hemingway project has re-examined the role of the common garden shed. Sheds have moved on from their traditional storage and potting area functions and can now serve as spare rooms, work spaces, reading areas or studios, all of which are much more lifestyle-orientated purposes. With £90 (US$138) million spent in the UK alone, the future of the 'garden' shed was clearly an area worthy of consideration. This is of course easy to say in hindsight, but recognising the change, spotting the opportunity and understanding the surrounding issues are all a part of the designer's imaginative function.

### ▶ Butt Butt for Straight PLC

A water barrel, known in the UK as a butt, here modelled as a butt! Aside from this pun, the butt has a flat front allowing it to be placed flat against a wall. It has a clear separation from traditional water barrels that will win it a unique target market.

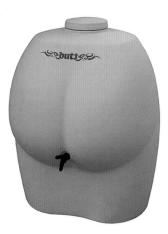

As a result, The Shackup range includes a small shed designed purely for bike storage and a range of sheds that combine traditional storage facilities with outdoor office space. This flexibility is enabled through a high roof height, large glazed areas and solid construction. The sheds are made from sustainable timber, which has a low carbon output that is not substantially raised if (as they are) parts are flat-packed. Hemingway provides the bike too. Another of his recent designs is the HD Roadrunner folding bike, which at around £60 (US$120) is one of the cheapest folding bikes on the market. Its affordability is such that it could realistically encourage more people to take up environmentally-efficient travel. To complement these socially and environmentally-aware products, Hemingway designed the Butt Butt, which has the advantage of being both a practical rainwater collection container and a fun, eye-catching feature in any garden (its unique feature being that it is in the shape of a human bottom).

The Shackup, HD Roadrunner and Butt Butt projects have to be seen in the context of the designer's interest in the way in which people interact, occupy and work with space and with each other. Hemingway does not have a formal education in product design and his ability to innovate across a variety of fields is a testament to the way in which a designer can identify and offer solutions for contemporary challenges through passion, a willingness to explore and reflect, an eye for detail and a drive to seize opportunities. Combined, Hemingway's ideas on architecture, space, living and travel represent a man striving to deliver his vision of the world.

### ▶ HD Roadrunner

This bike is designed to be the cheapest fold-up bike on the market and to provide an opportunity for householders to be able to afford, store and use a sustainable method of environmentally friendly transport.

A good designer seems able (if necessary) to cut across all of the practices, traditions and clutter of life to get to the heart of an issue. What's your secret?

**Wayne Hemingway**  Being able to identify problems, things that can be improved, gaps in the market … and, importantly, being dissatisfied with things and having a questioning mind – one that rarely shuts off.

You seem to have experimented with style and culture in your life. Do you think this helps?

**WH**  I started going out to clubs when I was 13, and grew up in the golden age of youth culture when we all experimented with soul, punk, rockabilly, ska, mod, new romantics. We dressed in the clothes, watched the films, researched the music … it had to help.

You have been able to find new ideas in the fashion, building, product and archiving industries. Do you find you need to adapt and change your ways of working?

**WH**  I've been very lucky in that I have had opportunity and freedom to go where I please. The basic ways of working don't change across the industry … identify need, understand customers, find a great team to help deliver, work bloody hard and market your concept wonderfully.

▶ **Bike store**
Hemingway's store is made from sustainable timber and designed to lend itself to bike storage, a concept that seems obvious, but is rarely seen in practice.

With Red or Dead, and the Land of Lost Content, you've forged your own path. Do you find working for clients such as B&Q, PURE and George Wimpey more restricting?

**WH**  More challenging, yes. It's harder in that there is a lot of cajoling, persuading, explaining and compromising to do, but we learn lots. It's an opportunity to reach a large new market and economies of scale help get our ideas to a wider audience. That's very important to us, it makes the brain work!

Do you ever look towards new materials and new technologies for inspiration?

**WH**  That's an integral part of being a designer. Having a knowledge of what's new and bringing that into your work.

You have taken a few risks in your career; do you ever worry that you are going to fail?

**WH**  There's always a chance of failure, but we have become good at balancing risk, and fortune favours the brave. As long as you set out on a project for the right reasons and put as much as possible into it as you can then failure is nothing to be ashamed of.

## ▶ The Shackup

A key concept behind the Shackup shed range is multifunctional purpose. It is tall, solid, and has large doors and window areas to maximise the flexibility of the space. It might feasibly be considered an external house extension rather than a traditional garden store. The shed shackle is a further element to the range that provides an additional level of security for shed contents, again recognising a social trend – this time, the increasing level of theft from garden areas.

# People's needs

Whilst a designer is capable of generating imaginative new product ideas, there are around six billion people in the world who have their own set of ideas about what they would like. Another way to generate product ideas is therefore to find out what these needs and wants are!

▶ **Wire Chair by Tom Dixon**
Inspired by the simple paperclip and designed to meet the needs of a specific market sector, this welded stainless steel wire chair can be used indoors or outdoors and forms part of a furniture series designed by Dixon that is based around the concept of lightweight but functional wire.
Photograph: Tom Dixon

### User-centred design

User-centred design is one way of describing a market-led approach to design. At the heart of this is the desire to understand what the core needs (or increasingly wants) of people are. Are these needs uniform or do they vary among similar people, or among different ages, genders or cultures? Conducting research in this way can enable new or better products to be identified and created.

A key issue here is that design-focused companies can target market information as a corporate strategy and manage and organise resources appropriately. This makes sense, as it is pointless to only occasionally release a new product if your competitors are regularly releasing new products with criteria that better meet the needs of the consumer. Design management is therefore an evolving subject area with issues of team working, information management, communication, branding and change. Designers, whether working within a company or for a company as a consultant, must recognise and work with these issues.

### Learning from market trends

An obvious place to start in understanding the market is to look at existing products to see how other designers are interpreting the market requirements. What sort of people are the products aimed at? What trends are there in the design? What are the differences in range, cost, material, shape and manufacturing processes? Which ones are more successful and why?

As well as products themselves, information can be gleaned from marketing reports or trade directory entries. This form of searching can be extensive, stretching to exploring a product's historic trends or related products and also might include political and economic considerations. For example, if you are selling a product such as a yacht to an American market, then you may want to know how buoyant the US economy is, what the exchange rates are doing and if any legislative trade changes are pending before deciding whether to design an upmarket version or not.

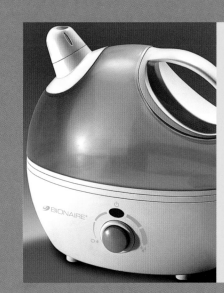

### ◀ Bionaire Compact Ultrasonic Humidifier

The blue colour and rounded features of this humidifier refers to a commonly accepted design style, but also makes it stand out from other products in Bionaire's range. Some organisations allow designers to develop individual styles, while others demand a 'house' style across their product range.

### ▶ The iMac by Apple Inc.

The iMac was introduced in 1998 and its curved form, translucent material and distinctive colours (such as the 'bondi blue' example shown here) stood it in stark contrast to the beige boxes that characterised most personal computers at that time. It was received by consumers and designers with critical acclaim; in fact, the effect has gone beyond the computer industry with companies inspired to innovate their own design classics.

Photograph: Apple Inc.

## Data collection

An empirical approach to market research is gathering first-hand data by asking people what they want. Techniques for this include interviewing, surveys, questionnaires and focus groups. It is not necessary to do this for every person that your product might be aimed at. Statistically, around 100 responses across a representative spread of people would give an approximate picture of the UK consumer market (roughly 58 million people) and a sample size of 1,000 should give a reasonably accurate picture.

It is, however, important to understand that weaknesses in data collection can lead to false answers with disastrous effects on the resulting product design. Weaknesses might include 'group think' in focus groups or asking leading questions in interviews. Good techniques are therefore essential, for example: iterate between 'how' and 'why' questioning to capture the emerging picture, cluster responses to find the route to the important parameters, force decisions rather than having 'don't know' or 'maybe' choices, and use 'should it be smaller, larger or stay the same' type questions to help the respondent.

I wore a colostomy bag for a week and I've also bought prosthetic breasts and tried on a bra. I've stabbed myself with injection devices and I've dressed up in surgical gear.
**Alun Wilcox (PDD)**

## Ethnography

Ethnography draws from the principles of anthropology (the study of humanity) in using research in the field to understand living cultures. Within product design, this translates to the belief that product knowledge can be gleaned from a designer's own empathy and experience. Designers can draw from their past experiences, or from new experiences established through situational testing such as role playing with specific products. This is a bit like method acting within the film industry where the 'actor' lives and feels a part before filming in order to understand the emotions of the character. Indeed, filming the experience and watching it over a number of times through the process of 'video ethnography' can reveal even more depth of understanding. It is, however, important to recognise that whilst ethnology is a rich area for understanding, on its own its results can be easily be tainted by our own prejudices and perceptual limitations.

## Observation

An understanding of the market can also be obtained by another anthropological technique, that of observation. In design, this means interpreting and understanding consumers' behaviour and decisions through their interaction with scenarios, products or prototypes. This can be done in situ (for example in homes or places of work), or as part of a specific test.

Behind the obvious activities may be deeper meanings of cognitive behaviour or cognitive human factors such as studying the absorption of information. Observations are therefore usefully recorded to allow events to be watched repeatedly for the detailed and subliminal clues and messages that may be involved.

Anthropology can provide an understanding into what product issues are, or an understanding of why current solutions may have failed. Testing methods, however, can be unscientific and open to inaccuracies or differing interpretations. For example, people who are being video recorded may change their behaviour simply because they are being recorded.

## Psychology and sociology

Psychology is the analytic and scientific study of mental processes and behaviour and includes concepts such as perception, cognition, emotion, personality, behaviour and interpersonal relationships. By attempting to understand the roles that these functions play, a designer may be able to design better products. Like observation, this can produce powerful, insightful information that people themselves might not recognise or be able to articulate through a direct interview. The design of a toy for a three-year-old child, for example, might be safer or more engaging if there is a greater understanding of a child's general cognitive and behavioural functions at that age.

Sociology offers an understanding of human needs in a working world context, through social or cultural interpretations. In this case, products are viewed very much as 'artefacts', having meaning and relevance to the world around them beyond pure function. A study of the semantics (meaning) and development in time of a product, or related products, might help to generate a better understanding of the product's underlying needs and requirements.

### ▶ Quinny Buzz pushchair

The Quinny Buzz looks striking and its design has met many of the needs gleaned from parents and infants – the product users. It has a seat that can be removed and used in the house or the car, it can also be used reversibly in the buggy itself so that the child can face forward or backwards. The buggy's unique triangular frame makes it lightweight, manoeuvrable and capable of unfolding automatically.

▶ **Hourglass Desk Clock**
(top right) **by David Dear
for Kikkerland, and
Rainbowmaker** (bottom
right) **by David Dear
for Kikkerland**

A graduate of Rhode Island
School of Design, David Dear
is one of many designers who
has made contributions to
Kikkerland Design's range
of products that bring witty,
novel or effective features
to mundane items with an
intrinsic appeal to many
consumers.

Dear's Hourglass clock
is most unusual; the red line
indicates the time, with the
minutes at the top, the hours
at the bottom, and seconds
indicated by the spinning disc
on the top. The Rainbowmaker
harnesses solar power to
rotate the crystal, and in
doing so refracts sunlight and
casts rainbows.

▲ **Sun Jar by Tobias Wong
for SUCK UK**

Seasonal affective disorder
(SAD) is a type of depression
that can be triggered by the
shortened daylight hours
of winter. Light therapy can
be an effective treatment for
SAD. Whilst not a therapy
itself, the Sun Jar does effect
a psychologically warming
experience. The jar collects
sunlight via a solar collector
and a battery and LED light
also provide a practical source
of light at night.

## ◄ Tube bus shelter

The Brazilian city of Curitiba pioneered Bus Rapid Transit (BRT) as a means of moving passengers around towns quickly and effectively. BRT systems include dedicated bus lanes, traffic signal priority and fare pre-payment as well as bus shelters that are raised to facilitate quicker bus entry and exit.

The tubular shapes of these bus shelters are in themselves inspiring and iconic. As a result of BRT, public transport – seen negatively in many car-rich cultures – is widely used as a matter of course by the majority of the city's two million inhabitants.

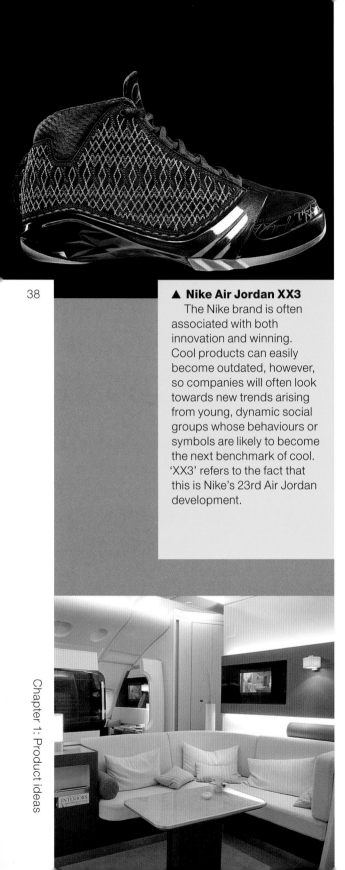

38

## ▲ Nike Air Jordan XX3

The Nike brand is often associated with both innovation and winning. Cool products can easily become outdated, however, so companies will often look towards new trends arising from young, dynamic social groups whose behaviours or symbols are likely to become the next benchmark of cool. 'XX3' refers to the fact that this is Nike's 23rd Air Jordan development.

## Cool hunting

Trends amongst younger age groups are important as they may become mainstream in the future. However, as the social groupings and subcultures of younger people become increasingly fragmented, it becomes harder to assess them with traditional research techniques such as questionnaires. It can also be difficult to assess a subculture if you do not understand it.

'Cool hunting' is a term that describes a combination of anthropological approaches such as living with sub-groups and observing with an understanding of sociology and psychology at work. Researchers should be outward, have a wide network of contacts and be capable of 'deep hanging out'. They should watch what young people are doing, where they are looking, what they are browsing, what badges they are wearing, how they are absorbing information, what communication methods are being used, what clothes and attitudes are displayed, and then interpret where these fads might go.

## Crowdsourcing

Whilst it is not necessary to ask everybody what they would like to see in a product in order to gain a perspective, of course the wider your survey the more accurate the results are likely to be. Usually, this is too expensive to undertake and there is a balance between sample size and risk to be struck. The Internet and web 2.0 technologies, however, have opened up opportunities for exploring a much wider range of opinions quickly and at low cost. Techniques might include email shots, websites and blogs, social networking sites or gaming sites such as Second Life. The neologism 'crowdsourcing' has been used to capture this method of working, although this sometimes refers specifically to the use of paid, off-site helpers rather than the general public (which is then referred to as 'opensourcing').

## Targeting

With six billion people in the world, it's unlikely that one design is going to meet the needs of everyone. Crucial decisions therefore have to be made as to who should and who should not be targeted. This does not mean forgetting the wider market and hoping that you don't make sales there, but it does mean undertaking the impossible task of trying to please everybody, because you won't be able to and will go mad in the process of trying to. Constructing a consumer profile for a typical member (or members) of your chosen market is helpful. This should include not just demographic data such as age and gender, but typical behavioural characteristics. It is the depth of knowledge behind these simple caricature presentations that makes this a very powerful technique.

In targeting specific markets, it is not uncommon to use standard definitions that help to segment the market into manageable and understandable sizes. These might include segments by lifestyle or newspaper readership, for example. The product idea you might aim at buyers of a low-cost, tabloid newspaper might be very different to a product aimed at more expensive broadsheet readers. A good product, however, is a good product – and it may be necessary to throw away these standard definitions and find new ways of looking at the market.

## Inclusive design

Often the decision to target a particular market is fundamentally an economic one, and normally the choice will select the people who will return the biggest profit to the product. There are exceptions though. For example, there are ethical reasons for making products that people with disabilities can engage with more easily, but there are economic reasons too. Improvements in medicine and welfare mean that there is a growing proportion of elderly or disabled people in society.

Inclusive, or universal, design incorporates many areas of good design practice including aesthetics and ergonomics. Design features generated might, for example, include comfortable handles, easy visual operational signs, strongly differentiated colours, and control through feel as well as sight. Many of these features will also appeal to the full spectrum of consumers and as such, inclusive design is not just designing for the disabled but also a philosophy aimed at addressing the needs of the widest possible audience; with principles that include equitability, simplicity, flexibility, intuitive and forgiving use, low effort and appropriate sizes and weights.

### ◄ Airbus A380

The A380 is the world's largest passenger airliner. However, it is a high-risk product that requires an Eu8 billion investment with no guarantee of any return. Why therefore take the chance of designing an interior that no one will like, or base decisions on small focus groups? Web 2.0 technology allows Airbus to canvas opinion on their design from anybody with access to the Internet.

# Matthew White

## Biography

Matthew White studied mechanical engineering before taking a course in industrial design engineering at the Royal College of Art, London and he now runs his own design practice in the south of England. Matthew is a good example of a user-centred designer who is capable of exploring all facets of a project, questioning many of the normal assumptions and traditions and producing products that make people look back and ask why these ideas weren't thought of before.

## Sandbug and Gofer screwdriver

Early in his career, B&Q (Europe's largest hardware chain store) asked Matthew to help the company in its quest to incorporate more inclusive products in its range. In order to better understand the needs of the do-it-yourself market, Matthew undertook a range of techniques that might best be described as 'action research'. Action research is a form of problem-solving that is based on a principle of oscillating between 'doing' and 'reflecting' to reach the optimum solution. It can be done individually or in groups and is a good technique to uncover new perspectives on the way that people and products interact.

A competitor product audit was undertaken first, followed by interviews conducted with B&Q customers and staff. As ideas were generated, two-hour long focus groups comprising five people each were conducted and prototypes were often used to help obtain both quantitative and qualitative feedback. Further feedback was obtained through user testing, a process involving the assessment of users as they performed specific tasks with various tools, test concepts and prototypes. These were again discussed in informal focus groups. Over a period of eight months, nine users were selected and given a range of tools and tasks, in order to evaluate and feedback on both existing tools and new ideas. Key issues from the action research were then written into the product brief.

### ◄ Sandbug

Matthew White was aided by the Helen Hamlyn Research Centre (HHRC) on this project with B&Q to design power tools that could be used by older people with reduced grip. Users guide the Sandbug sander by palm rather than having to hold a handle.

Matthew's subsequent ideas included separating the heavy batteries from power tools so that these could be carried independently; making the drill lighter so it could be handled easily by the less physically able. He questioned why it was that screwdrivers were invariably long and thin, a shape that can be particularly hard for elderly people to hold. White's screwdriver, the Gofer, is designed in a pebble-like shape: smooth and rounded so that it fits into a hand more easily. It also has an electric drive to aid one-handed screwing. Unlike most electric screwdrivers, it is designed with a 'push and go' mechanism instead of a button.

White also redesigned a sanding device so that it would be easier to hold. The Sandbug features a large domed body that fits into a cupped hand and has a generous hand strap for extra grip (the inspiration for these design details came from observing people using a horse brush).

The Gofer and the Sandbug do not resemble traditional tools, but, like many inclusive designs, their features appeal to a much wider audience than just the elderly or less able, making them highly successful products.

▲ **Gofer screwdriver**
By providing new products such as the Gofer screwdriver, B&Q can score an advantage over its DIY-store competitors and achieve a new innovation-related brand image. 'Innovation' and 'user-friendly' become the key words to describe the Gofer's design.

◀ **Sandbug and Gofer screwdriver**

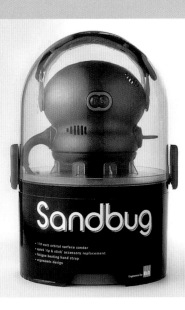

## Q&As

Innovation always seems so easy – with the benefit of hindsight! How do you go about generating ideas for new products?

**Matthew White** I look at the state of the current products (if they exist) and often try them and take them apart. Then I sketch and think a lot. I try out ideas simply and go from there. I try to really think about the actual use of a product and then am inspired to give the end-user the product they need.

You are very strong in determining what people need from a product. How do you ensure that your own prejudices don't interfere with the way concepts are developed?

**MW** They always do – let them! The best thing to do is be prejudiced in the right way – to think like people who struggle with products or who aren't being catered for yet. But I still fall into the trap of designing for myself. To avoid this, you have to interact with users as much as possible during development – even if just a friend or colleague.

Have you changed the way that you do your research, either over time or for different products?

**MW** Yes – it varies a lot depending on budget. The Sandbug and Gofer were all about research with those less able. It's not always practical to do a lot, but important to do it once and carry those experiences with you.

Any ideas how we might define cool?

**MW** Yes – in many ways 'cool' just means it's the way it should be – or rather feels like it should be. It doesn't stand out as poor design or a try-hard!

Which other designers do you admire and draw inspiration from?

**MW** Difficult. I don't actually spend much time looking at others' work. I think you can try to just emulate them too much. Names that stand out for me are Stark and Lovegrove but that's quite obvious! I tend to let individual objects and pieces of design inspire me – the Bird's Nest stadium [in China] really has recently.

Is it easy to sell new ideas to the client companies you work for?

**MW** It's easy to get interest and some enthusiasm but far harder to keep it over the long term of product development. As budget and time increases, the sell becomes harder and harder. There is a real hunger for innovative products, though, more so than for beautiful products.

# Chapter summary

This chapter has explored two different ways of generating ideas for products. One involves a personal way of looking at products through a series of ideas that revolve around individuality, independence of thought, reflection and empathy. The second way involves looking at the needs of others by exploring the marketplace. The skills required can be more analytical, technical and open to agreement, making it a more transparent process (akin to a 'white box' design method as opposed to a more concealed 'black box' method).

Which is the better method to use? Both are open to some criticism. Free-thinking designers can insist on following their own visions, which may be prejudiced or jaundiced or lead to products that only the designer likes and have no real purpose or demand. A market-led approach may conversely be driven by people with no idea of what might be achievable, resulting in bland and boring products.

Creating new product ideas might therefore require a mixture of both approaches, with designers requiring an ability to create new products from the imagination, and/or an ability to detect product needs from within the marketplace. Generating new product ideas can therefore be described as both an art and a science and this diversity in design thinking is at once one of the beauties and challenges of design.

### Exercise 1

Subverting or adapting everyday products can lead to new product ideas. Sometimes it's necessary to do this because the original purpose of the product is less successful than planned. Swarfega, the green gunk that cleans dirty workshop hands, for example, started life as a failed protective barrier for products such as metal and silk stockings.

Construct a list of everyday products and artefacts and try to adapt these for sensible, but completely different, uses.

### Exercise 2

Some of the findings attributed to coolhunting techniques include the statements that 'the more developed a culture becomes, the more eccentric it gets' and that 'everyone wants to keep his or her option open'.

Keeping these two statements in mind, consider how you might redesign a domestic kitchen waste bin.

**◀ Dahlia by Janne Kyttänen for Freedom of Creation**

Danish designer Janne Kyttänen's light is made from laser-sintered polyamide and, as the product's name suggests, was inspired by the mathematics and layout of nature's dahlia flower.

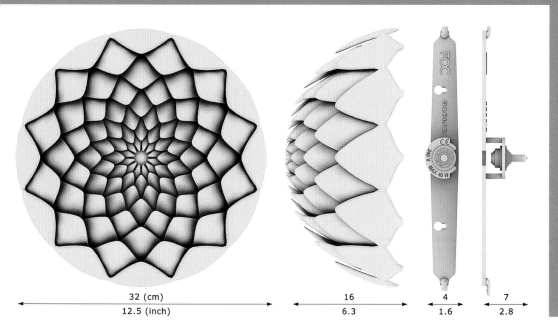

| 32 (cm) | 16 | 4 | 7 |
| 12.5 (inch) | 6.3 | 1.6 | 2.8 |

# The product brief

My job is to make our products obsolete before our competitors do.
**Akito Morito, Sony Chairman**

**One of the key factors behind successful innovation is the ability to first generate a good idea and then capture it by turning it into an accurate product brief. It is the brief that dictates the way in which the design will develop.**

**The product brief outlines the broad requirements, notional concepts, initial scope and constraints. There is a debate as to whether the brief should be narrow and descriptive, or broad and vague. One argument is that truly agile enterprises should start with specifications that are as wide as possible as they will be imaginative and capable of adapting to new ideas. Either way, the brief should contain enough information to define the concept, but not constrain the subsequent development.**

◄ **Leatherman® Skeletool**

# Defining needs

This section explores the early-stage thinking that takes a vague concept for a new product idea and turns it into something more tangible. It is a vital stage in the design process; getting this wrong will commit time, money and resources to an expensive and ultimately flawed development stage.

Surveys suggest that the innovative ability of many organisations is actually quite low. Sometimes this is obvious, with products that look poor or work badly, but such products are usually quickly pulled from the market. The real damage of poorly executed products is hidden in the cost of those that take too long to get to the market, those that allow better ones from competitors to take a bigger market share and those that necessitate an expensive redesign.

▶ **BeoLab 5 by Bang & Olufsen**
Some companies might consider technical excellence as their priority market criteria, whilst others might select innovation or style. Bang & Olufsen attempt to satisfy all of these criteria across their range of speakers and electrical products and are largely successful in doing so. The BeoLab 5 loudspeaker (shown in the foreground) is enormously powerful and, with its circular cone design, can be placed anywhere in a room.

## Criteria

Criteria are the descriptors that define a product's requirements. It is preferable to write these down as an aid to clarity and a way of communicating the product requirements to a larger audience. It can be common to find these criteria written as rather loose descriptions, for example, 'the product should be big', but in reality this is not helpful. 'Big' to one person may be small to another, and how can you determine whether your finished product is big enough? It is therefore often helpful to define criteria precisely using (where possible) quantifiable metrics.

Design can be a breathtakingly wide activity and whilst this can be invigorating and exciting, it can be challenging too, requiring the simultaneous handling of complex, and sometimes conflicting, demands and information. For example, if a product needs to be both lightweight and durable then there may come a point in the design process where making it lighter begins to make its lifetime shorter. As such, it's important to establish at the outset if some of the product's criteria are more important than others.

By prioritising, designers can put the right emphasis on the most important criteria area and have some clarity when difficult decisions have to be made.

## Market criteria

Unique selling points (USPs) relate to a product's key propositions and strengths.

**Market-qualifying criteria** are attributes that the customer expects from all competing products. **Order-losing criteria** are those considered to be critical to the customer, and products that fail to include them will exclude the supplier from consideration.

**Order-winning criteria** are those attributes that enable a company's products to gain an advantage over their competitors in the eyes of the customers.

Japanese theorist Ayako Kano considered that criteria could also be categorised into expected features (basic), features that increase customer satisfaction as they improve (one dimensional) and non-expected features that differentiate the product (exciters).

## Product range

Another decision that needs to be made at this early stage is whether one product will meet the market need or whether a range of products is required. This can depend heavily on how varied the market is. For example, a straightforward market with uniform needs may be satisfied by a single product, but a complex market – one with wide-ranging tastes, cultures and requirements – may require a range of products to be generated. The differentiation in a range of products might include simple choices about colour, to more complex decisions about sizing, performance and the modularity of a design.

## Benchmarking

Sometimes it's easy to get caught up in the excitement of a new idea and a potential new development. Benchmarking is the name given to the process of comparing and evaluating your position against that of others, and this can bring a sense of reality to the design challenge ahead. Reverse engineering of your competitor products is one technique that can be used and is particularly useful in appraising the technical levels and standards that an industry is working to. Benchmarking can be a useful tool in defining the needs of your market audience.

No manufacturer, from General Motors to the Little Lulu Novelty Company, would think of putting a product on the market without benefit of a designer.
**Raymond Loewy**

▶ **Leatherman® Skeletool**

For many years, Swiss army knives have been the acknowledged benchmark against which other penknives might be measured. The Leatherman® series has introduced new materials, tools and ideas in a way that has redefined the benchmark. No longer a knife with accessory tools, the benchmark might now be considered as a multitool that includes blades.

▶ **USBCELL USB rechargeable batteries by Moixa Energy Ltd.**

These may look like standard rechargeable AA batteries, but removing the end cap reveals a connector, which enables the batteries to be recharged through a computer's USB port. It's an innovative idea, removing the need to have a standard battery charger and providing people with a chance to charge batteries wherever they find themselves working. It adds another option to a range of batteries available on the market.

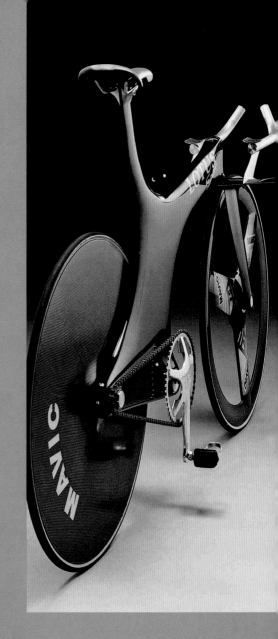

**▲ Sorapot teapot by Joey Roth**

The simple criteria that a teapot could be expected to meet might include an ability to keep water hot and to provide a safe and simple pouring capability. The elegant structure and clear viewing of the Sorapot, made from 304 stainless steel and borosilicate glass, might meet a more developed set of criteria such as the need to provide a visual stimulus or to emphasise the ritual of the tea-making process.

◀ **LotusSports Pursuit Bicycle by Mike Burrows**

The modern diamond-shaped bicycle frame was once thought to be the pinnacle of bike design, yet a combination of new analytical techniques, materials and manufacturing technologies has allowed yet further innovation.

Mike Burrows designed a carbon-fibre, moulded monocoque-framed bike as an alternative to the more traditional steel-tubed bike in the 1980s, but the design was turned down by bike manufacturers and rejected by the cycling regulatory bodies. A rule change in 1990, however, meant that the bike could be considered 'legal' and the design was taken up by Lotus (who have particular expertise with carbon-fibre design and manufacture).

**Incremental and quantum innovation**

Large-scale innovations, representing quantum leaps in thinking and design, are undoubtedly exciting and there are many examples of inventions that have changed and sometimes shaken the world. These might range from digital radios to satellites, from mobile phones to memory sticks and Tetra Pack cartons to hybrid cars.

Organisations that release a radical new product are shown to maintain a significant market share over a long period of time, even after competitors catch up and release 'me-too' products. There are other long-term benefits too, including spin-off products, a culture of wanting more success and a goodwill factor with the public for being seen as innovative.

Normally, radical innovation is the result of a design team hard at work within a commercial organisation. Individuals within that team, such as associated consulting organisations or designers, are all capable of reaping the kudos that radical and successful new products bring. This is often the dream of both new and experienced designers alike.

Whilst it is important for all designers to seek to innovate, it is equally important to recognise that it is not always possible to generate radically new ideas; as few as five per cent of new products released into the market each year are actually considered radically 'new'. Instead, most newly-released products represent minor variations on previous themes or copies of other ideas (these are usually referred to as 'me-too' products).

It's very easy to be different,
but very difficult to be better.
**Jonathan Ive**

▶ **Smart Crossblade**
The concept and technology for the Smart Car is clear: it's a small urban car, but it's not sensible simply to make a big car smaller, so the specification for this type of car requires attention to issues of comfort, space and economy. To meet these specifications, the Smart Car is lightweight and has almost cubic dimensions that give it extra internal space and stability.

### Feasibility

An issue for designers is to know just how far into the realms of impossibility to go before it becomes pure science fiction. A product might be 'makeable' now, 'makeable' in the very near future, 'makeable' in the distant future, or just a distant dream. The rate of change in technology makes it very difficult to predict just how far to set the criteria and sometimes tough decisions have to be made about whether to use known and existing technology or to risk trying something new or unanticipated.

### Product design specification

A product design specification draws together and summarises thoughts, research, imagination and data and in doing so, turns the outline proposal or conceptual brief into a more detailed statement. This should not be confused with a technical specification, which is a description of the completed product and its characteristics.

The product design specification should define what the completed product should aim to do. As such, it provides clarity for everybody involved in the product's future development. It also acts as a catalyst and a reality check between all stakeholders. It might not only clarify what is known as being required, but may also outline what is not known and needs further work.

# Emmanuel Laffon de Mazières

## Biography

Emmanuel Laffon de Mazières graduated from the Institut Supérieur de Design in Valenciennes, France with a postgraduate degree in engineering design management. He has worked as an intern at IDEO and with companies One & Co and Fuseproject. Emmanuel's philosophy is to bring the process of design back to the more intimate relationship between designer and user and move away from the barriers between designer and customer thrown up by industrialisation and mass production and consumption.

## The Huit Sofa

Designed in 2007, the Huit Sofa is an example of a designer striving to interpret quite subtle emotions and issues and translate them into a product. Technically, a 'love seat' might be defined as any seating arrangement that places two people in close proximity; from a simple two-seat settee or couch, through to a dome, laid-back arrangements or complex intertwining configurations.

As such, the Huit Sofa is an addition to the thousands of designs in the love seat category, but its achievement suggests that the designer has managed to define and capture a significant market rationale. When asked about this rationale Emmanuel comments that:

'If we talk only about the semantic aspect, the strength of this product speaks for itself. The basic idea of the product is a two-dimensional shape turned into a three-dimensional [one]. Originally it's inspired by an '8' shape, but some people also see the symbol for infinity too. I wanted to express the infinity of love and actually, "love seat" is the technical term for this kind of sofa, but being French I didn't even know this when I designed it. It's interesting to see that some people have an interpretation of your design that you didn't think about.'

'I tried also to play around with several things: the top (red) ribbon is enhanced in order to make a relation between the two people who can fit in it. The idea is that this ribbon is almost floating into air as the rest of the sofa (white) visually disappears. When you turn the sofa around, the shape drawn by this ribbon in the space is always new, surprising and elegant. According to your point of view, the shape is never the same.'

## ► Huit Sofa

The Huit Sofa is a concept piece of furniture that is designed in the shape of an infinity symbol. The continuous curves flow in such a way that when seated in different positions on the sofa, your point of view is never the same.

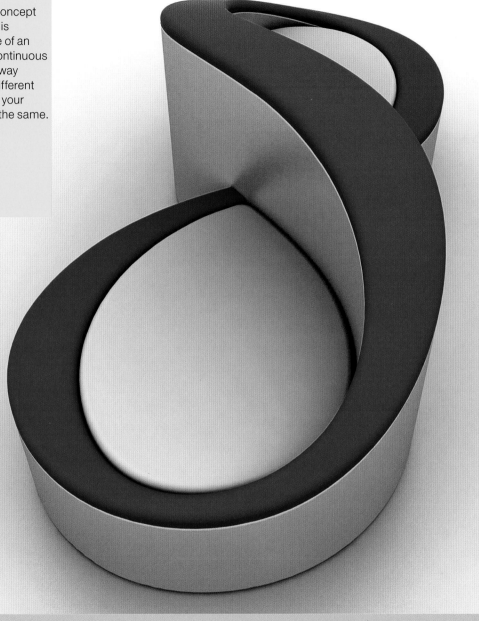

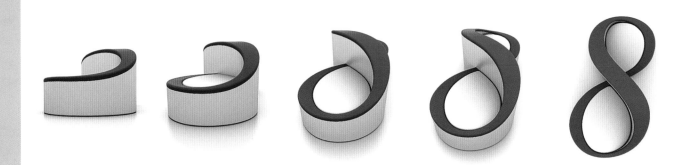

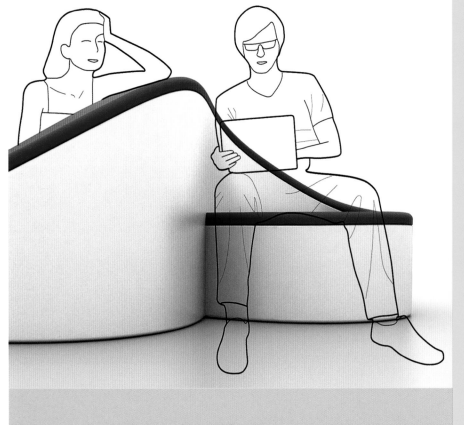

### ◀ Huit Sofa

It is unlikely that many designers, if presented with a list of client needs, would have conjured up the Huit Sofa as a direct response. In this case, the design encompasses the development of two different ideas: the number '8' and the functional requirements of a settee have combined to create cascading compartments and features.

Listing needs is a good way of clarifying thoughts and testing ideas for further consideration. Needs listing is particularly valuable for communication in large design teams and for highlighting the key issues that need to be addressed.

**Q&As**

What made you think about using
a figure of 8 in the first place?

**Emmanuel Laffon de Mazières**
I always liked the number 8, not because I
am superstitious but for aesthetic reasons.
I like this closed shape, the proportions
and I find its curves when it is typed
very sensual. My design was actually an
experience; what would happen if I take
a typed number and tried to give it a third
dimension? I found out that this shape has
the property to create two intimate spaces
and were ideal for a love seat. Usually
in the design process, you try to solve
a problem with a shape. Here I did the
opposite it was quite fun.

How do you develop your awareness
of what people want in a product?

**ELdM** A good designer is someone
who has an overdeveloped sense of
observation and empathy. Observation
because creating is all about having your
eyes wide open to people's behaviours
and needs, but also to technological
progress and cultural trends. Empathy
because most of the products I design
are intended for other people, whose
fundamental needs and dreams I need
to understand.

Do you think there are wide-ranging
differences in what people want, say
between cultures, genders or ages,
or could a good product cut across
all the divides?

**ELdM** I fundamentally believe that a
good product cuts across all the different
cultures. Design is like art: it is partially
cultural, but it is also a universal language.
I wrote a little book called *Iconic Design*
where I explain that good industrial design
is all about finding this very language; the
pictures that refer deeply to our common
culture and memory.

What other designers do you admire
and think are really able to gauge what
people want?

**ELdM** I think people often do not
always know what they want and a big
error made by companies when designing
a product is to ask the customers what
they want. It's like an artist making a survey
about people's favourite colours before
starting a painting! A good designer is able
to catch in the air what's hot and translate
this into a good design. Customers today
need to be surprised and it is all about
speaking the right language. My favourite
designers are the Bouroullec brothers
and Naoto Fukasawa. I like the Bouroullec
brothers for their deep sense of colour,
curves and the magical poetry that beams
from their objects. Fukasawa is able to
remove everything that is not absolutely
necessary to reach the very essence of
his products. Design today is a lot about
adding more stuff and features. I like his
designs because there is a lot less, and
this makes my soul rest and available for
more important things.

# Market trends

In trying to understand how to define a product, it can be interesting and useful to look at the current market trends to see where you are and to know where the world is going. There are both seasoned and contemporary factors that can influence market trends. This section explores some of these trends.

### **Individuality and rebellion**

As the population grows and systems, technology and organisations take more and more control of our lives, it is easy to feel dwarfed and swamped by the massed but 'invisible' forces around us. One reaction to this is a need to feel unique amongst the morass all around. This reaction also occurs in design and is evidenced by an increasing consumer demand for varied ranges and the rapid turnover of fashion and products. It is also evident in the process of selecting products or brands that we feel will help to define us: do you want to carry an iPod or a Walkman? Wear Nike or Converse? Drive a Volkswagen or a Fiat?

Taken a step further, it is argued that consumerism is driven by the desire to find not just individuality, but personal happiness through the purchase of material possessions. Social commentators such as Karl Marx were noting as long ago as the nineteenth century that there was a shift from consumption to meet people's 'needs' to consumption to meet society's 'wants'.

Counterculture is a response to our increasing societal and consumer demands and incorporates movements that seek to oppose the economic and political frameworks that are seen to create life's stresses and strains. These movements range from 'TV Turnoff week' to 'Reclaim the Streets' to Adbusters. Countercultural movements might even be considered anti-cool. The rebellion response within design might include generating simple, low-cost and non-branded products, or products that are socially and community orientated.

### **Customisation**

Based on a precept of individuality, an emerging market trend has been to provide products that can be customised by their owners, giving consumers feelings of empowerment and satisfaction through realising their own unique product. It's a form of 'pimp my product' and clip-on mobile phone covers, products with programmable open-source software and products with gel form coatings that change shape over time with use are some examples of this in practice.

I think that good designers must always be avant-gardists, always one step ahead of the times.
**Dieter Rams**

## ▶ Do hit chair for Droog by Marijn van der Poll

Nike's 'consumer decides' philosophy is a strategic direction taken by the company that allows customers to design their own footwear. It's driven by the acknowledgement that an 18-year-old has different tastes and demands even to that of a 22-year-old.

This demand for individualism is a significant design trend, but mocked here with Droog's typical dry humour by the Do hit chair. Designed by Marijn van der Poll, the Do hit chair is one that can be fashioned by the owner smashing, hitting and pounding it into shape (using the sledgehammer provided with the purchase).

Photographs: Robbard/Theuwkens (styling by Marjo Kranenborg (top) and Gerard van Hees (bottom))

## Cool

'Cool' is a difficult word to define, but one attempt at it might be the gaining of expressions of admiration from peers. But why do people need to be cool? The need for peer approval may derive from a simplistic instinct to be accepted, in order to be safe and to be able to succeed, but this instinct may become more powerful as a result of the complexities and pressures of our modern world.

One way to be 'cool' might be to have the latest admired product, or a range of highly-regarded products, since this might indicate your willingness to spend money to be a part of your peer group and your ability to make good decisions. The inference for designers might therefore be to make high-value or high-performing products.

## Organic

If you look at the products around you now, you may find it hard to find anything that is perfectly square. If you are sitting at your desk, look at the lamp, your mouse, a pen or the telephone; how many perfectly straight lines are incorporated in these products?

The trend for smooth, curving organic shapes is in some cases a reaction and shift away from the clean, symmetric designs of earlier years. In other ways, it mirrors nature and natural forms, where few straight edges can be found. Organic lines can give products a more natural aesthetic and feel to them and computer-aided surface and solid modelling, coupled with advances in manufacturing techniques, has facilitated this trend.

## NURBS

Designers have been quick to enjoy the many possibilities that advances in manufacturing techniques and computer technologies have provided. NURBS (non uniform rational basis spline) are mathematical models inside computer graphics and design packages that allow flexible, free-form curves and surfaces to be generated easily and effectively using control points. French engineers Beziér and de Casteljau pioneered these techniques, as evidenced in the curved shapes of Renault and Citroen cars of the 1960s.

### ▶ Napshell

The Napshell has been developed by seven architecture students at the University of Stuttgart to aid and legitimise power napping, a social habit that varies from country to country, but that is believed to promote creativity and health.

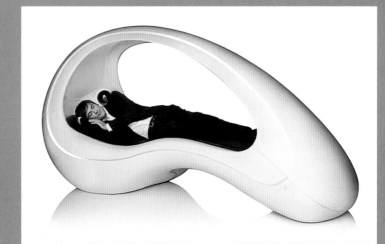

▶ **iRobot® Scooba® 385
Floor Washing Robot**

Some people like technology just for the sake of it. Others adopt a more practical rationale in order to achieve, for example, more security, better communications capability, status or earning potential. This automated floor cleaner removes a chore that not only takes up time, but is probably considered very dull by most people.

Photographs: iRobot®

### ▲ Gas Grill by Eva Solo

As people have placed more importance on their free time and made more effective use of their time, then leisure products have assumed an increasingly important role in society. Eva Solo's range of simple, pure stainless steel and ceramic barbecue equipment brings an added dimension of pleasure to outdoor cooking and socialising.

### Technology

Some people may like technology in its own right. Many more may like the benefits that come from technological advances. Consider a mobile phone. Some consumers may buy it because it has numerous clever functions, some may buy it and only use a few of those functions and some people may simply dislike the social intrusion that mobile phones can bring and not buy one at all.

There is an enormous amount of literature written about technology. Is it a good thing that brings new experiences and promotes a labour-saving world? Is it a bad thing that brings exploitation, environmental damage and social and physical dangers? Quite often product designers will be technically adept and motivated, but it is important to recognise that there is another side to the technology argument.

### Legitimise

Products that legitimise the user's behaviour may be more acceptable and less obvious than confrontational products. For example, personal music players with earphones offer a means of shutting away the noise, intrusions and dramas of the outside world while the listener enjoys a period of legitimate, restful calm.

### Play and leisure

If being individual, cool, or rebellious are reactions to a pressured social environment, then products that help to relieve those pressures are to be welcomed. Play has a powerful way to achieve this and a designer might aim to develop products that not only perform a function, but help people to let off steam, de-stress, smile and laugh. There are numerous examples of these, from the ironic products of Alessi to the simple jokes on the cartons of Innocent smoothies ('shake before opening, not after').

Leisure activities have a similar function to play in allowing people to de-stress and, where the leisure pursuit is active, there is a detoxing benefit too. Many people are also exploring different leisure activities to previous generations, allowing for further design scope. Mountain bikes, reading lights, social networking sites, parkour and DIY might represent some of the developments in leisure style products.

### Kidults

There is growing recognition that children are trying to grow up quickly and adults are trying to become more childlike. The term 'kidult' has been used to describe this phenomenon, and the consequences of this trend on design are less subtle than just designing products with a playful edge. The effect is to design adult products for children and children's toys for adults.

A designer might therefore produce small, working versions of adult things rather than simplified, toy-like replicas for children (such as a small metal toolkit in a toolbox rather than a blow-moulded set in a plastic bag). Educational toys have similarly become the largest growth sector in the toy market, particularly for electronic products such as miniature laptops. Electronic games are also a growth area for adults and, along with novelty kitchen gadgets, amateur DIY versions of professional tools and quad bikes, might all represent adult versions of children's toys and hobbies.

### Tactility

Design is often (incorrectly) thought of as a purely visual practice, but touch and feel can be equally important. Look around you and you rarely see people that are not doing something with their hands – holding bags, tapping pencils, touching their hair. This somasensory feedback from touch is stimulating and memorable, and therefore incorporating it into products is a valuable activity. Smoothness is one aspect. Shot or sandblasting die moulds give plastic its familiar stipled texture whilst metalised plastic has a smoother, friction-reduced finish. Shape, thickness and thermal conductivity can have an equal role in the tactile experience. Developments in gel and polymer coatings similarly provide rich areas for designers to explore.

▶ **iPhone by Apple**
The iPhone is smooth and solid with a breathtaking user-centric touchscreen control. Whilst its performance and cost have been the subject of some discussion, the iPhone's combination of touch sensitivity and functionality have made it a beautifully tactile and consequently outstanding product for many people.
Photograph: Apple Inc.

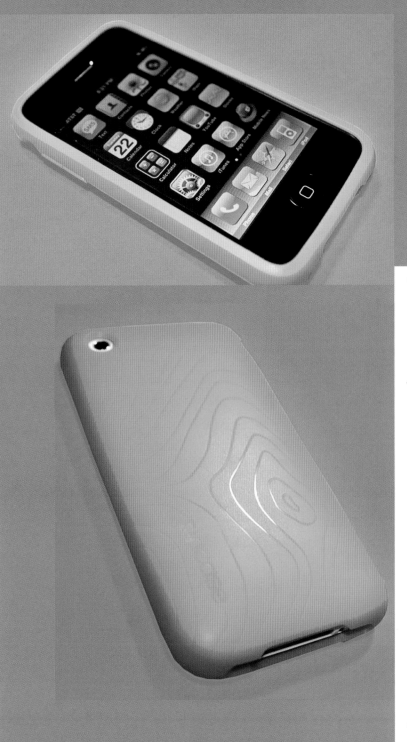

### ▶ Protective cover for iPhone by Incase

This product rebels against Apple's smooth white iPhone by providing a contoured and coloured covering.

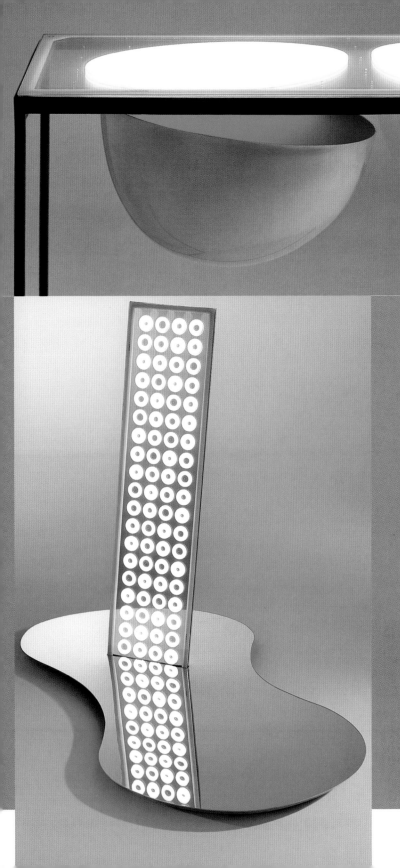

◀ **Lightpieces by SAAZS co-developed with Saint-Gobian Innovations**

The SAAZS lightpieces range incorporate light-emitting glass that uses the glass itself to generate light that is uniformly even with a temperature close to that of the human body so that it can be touched safely. The LightBird (a coffee table and a lamp) has a similar soothing effect, using varnished steel to create a velvet-like texture into which pure but warm light patterns are floated. Flaq is a lighting piece of furniture and a sculpture. Flying dots is a bookshelf and Balafon is a console.

**LightBird by Tomas Erel** (facing page, top)**; Flaq by Tomas Erel** (this page, bottom)**; Flying dots (detail) by Christain Biecher** (facing page, bottom) **and Balafon by Adrien Gardère** (this page, top)

Photographs: Jean-François Le Sénéchal (LightBird); Saaza-DR (Flaq) and Morgane Le Gall (Flying dots and Balafon)

**▲ Formway PLI chair**

This furniture series uses a plywood shell and a brushed stainless-steel leg frame to provide a lightweight, but comfortable and long-lasting chair. Water-based, CFC-free foams and sustainable timber are also used. The simplicity and longevity contribute to the provision of an environmentally friendly, low-energy product.

**◄ Knotted Chair by Marcel Wanders**

This armchair is made of macramé knotted carbon and aramide fibre cord with an epoxy resin finish. Whilst the materials might not be considered environmentally friendly, it is a good example of achieving an environmentally friendly product through low material content.

Photograph: Cappellini
Courtesy of
Marcel Wanders Studio
www.marcelwanders.com

## Sustainability

The term 'sustainable development' was defined by the World Commission report on Environment and Development (the 1987 Brundtland Commission) as 'development that meets the needs of the present without compromising the ability of future generations to meet their own needs'. Sustainability therefore encompasses broad concepts of economics and politics in addition to its more familiar environmental considerations.

## Environmental concerns

Concerns about the environment have been raised since the 1950s when an increasing number of people began to question the assumption that the earth could accommodate and absorb all human activity. Only recently has it been widely accepted that human activity is having a negative effect on the planet (deriving largely from the Intergovernmental Panel on Climate Change report of February 2007 involving 600 scientists from 133 countries). Product design and product designers are thought to play a significant role in environmental impact issues.

This late agreement has meant environmentally friendly products have been quite slow to appear on the market, but there is now a trend towards creating 'greener' products. New ideas and technologies are emerging to help designers make the necessary breakthroughs in producing more environmentally friendly products.

# Luigi Colani

### Biography

Luigi Colani is a maverick industrial designer, with a walrus moustache and a proclivity for white suits and large cigars. He was born in Germany in 1928 and studied sculpture in Berlin and aerodynamics at the Sorbonne in Paris, subsequently working with or for companies such as McDonell-Douglas, Fiat, BMW, Mazda and Sony. His collaborations are reputed to cover over 5000 industrial and consumer products and range from cars, planes and trains through to computers, headphones, cosmetics, sunglasses and uniforms. Colani and his team have won many awards and achieved many 'firsts' for their work including the BMW 700 sports car and the Canon T90 camera. Colani is considered by many to be one of the world's most influential designers.

### Bucking the trend

Whilst Colani's list of products and awards is impressive it is perhaps his style for which he is best known. His 'biodynamic' or 'biomorphic' style is characterised by rounded, organic forms that incorporate a heavy acknowledgement of nature. Colani refers to himself as a three-dimensional philosopher and asks why he should join the straying masses and make everything angular.

Colani's style has often been too challenging, too futuristic or too grand to be accepted by everyone and his larger designs are often not taken up at all, but this is of little concern to the man himself, who is keen to impress his willingness to experiment.

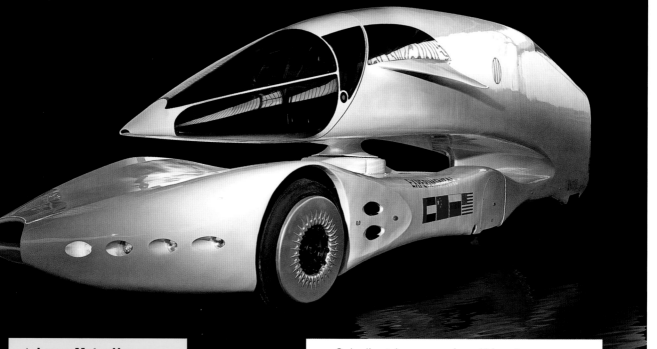

**▲ Luxus Motor Home**
A streamlined motor home concept.

**◄ Poly-COR-Chair**
A plastic chair that draws on the single leg design of Eero Saarinen, but incorporates a cantilever feature. Difficult to produce, but this 1968 design remains relevant today.

Colani's style, approach and ideas have numerous supporters who straddle both the eastern and western hemispheres. He has equally influenced a generation of designers with interests in anatomy, technology and bioforms. Designers such as Ross Lovegrove and Karim Rashid might all cite Colani as a major source of inspiration. It is an influence that is seemingly gaining more advocates because whilst the feats of other designers and design groups might fade over time, Colani's work seems even more relevant to today's markets than ever. Tactile materials, technology and anthropomorphism, fluid curves enabled by modern CAD software and environmentally driven calls are all highly visible trends in today's products, but all of these issues are evident throughout Colani's 50-year body of work. There might even be a debate as to whether Colani's work predicts market trends, meets them, or actually sets them.

# Product requirements

A product needs to be defined not just by a designer's ideas or by consumer requirements, but by other considerations too. There is, for example, a particular need to undertake a form of due diligence in order to establish any operational requirements, whether these relate to performance, safety, legal or regulatory functions. These should be captured within the product design specification. There is also a need to engage with these information gathering processes in a manner that is both thorough and quick because of the speed at which data changes and because competitors will take advantage of any hesitation.

### Regulations

Trade organisations, umbrella groups or controlling authorities may set rules and guidelines for the design and manufacture of some products. An example of these is the minimum performance requirements set by the International Organization for Standardization (the ISO). The ISO is a non-governmental body (to which most of the industrialised world's countries are affiliated) that sets industrial and commercial standards.

Some of the ubiquitous ISO standards that designers will commonly engage with include the 14000 series on environmental management systems and the 9000 series on quality management systems. Most countries will in addition have their own national standards authority that will interpret ISO standards or may develop their own complementary or alternative standards. For example, the British Standard BS7000 is a guide to systems for managing the design process.

Innovative new products may push the boundaries faster than these administrative bodies can work and this is particularly evident in sport or IT industries where the introduction of new ideas can challenge and overwhelm existing rules and regulations.

### Legislation

Through treaties or interpretation by national bodies, many ISO standards will in fact become statutory requirements. Governments may also have their own additional legal requirements that designers must adhere to. In European Union (EU) legislation, for example, the New Approach Directives are aimed at specific products such as toys, sports or safety equipment.

Similarly, there may be rules on costs, materials used, environmental protection, methods of fixing, labelling or notifications of goods for export, and all of these legal requirements must be included in the product specification. Since products may be exported anywhere in the world, designers should work to the appropriate legislation and not just that of their own country.

The European Economic Area (EEA) requires some products to be 'CE' or 'conformance marked' to show that they have been produced according to the relevant directives and legislation.

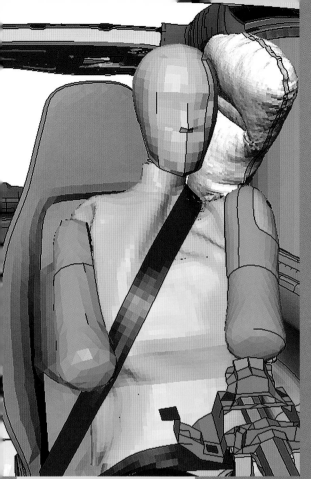

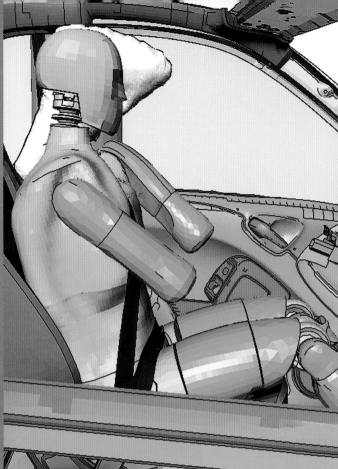

### ▶ Smart Car

The cubic design of the Smart Car could make it vulnerable to impact damage in a collision. To overcome this, the car has a hemishperical steel shell that provides safety for occupants and also forms the car's chassis.

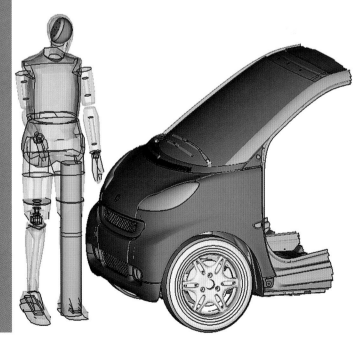

### ▶ The Safe Sippy

There is some concern over the use of plastic in product design. For example, polycarbonate uses Bisphenol A, a chemical that has the capacity to do harm to the human body. This concern is particularly relevant to food wrapping and drinks bottle designs, especially for young children. Evidence is, however, difficult to assess and consequently regulations are unclear.

The Safe Sippy overcomes any doubt because it is made from stainless steel, which avoids any possible toxic leaching of material into a child's drink. It also has a sleeve to help the steel from being dented and to keep the bottle at a comfortable temperature to hold.

Photographs:
The Safe Sippy/Kid Basix

## Safety

There are of course ethical reasons for not wishing to be responsible for injury to consumers, but most countries have defined some notion of 'safe' product-making, which makes it illegal to sell a product that is intrinsically dangerous. The product specification should include the minimum requirements that would deem a product safe and the levels to which the product might go beyond these. A designer should therefore consider the minimum safety standards and safety factors to work to. An example of this might be the maximum load that the user might be able to lift or hold.

Designers assume that if a design meets the performance levels set by regulations and guidelines then it might automatically be considered a safe product, but this is untrue. Some designers also only consider their target market when considering safety factors when, in fact, the user might be a young child, or an elderly or infirm user with a different level of ability.

A common mistake that people make when trying to design something completely foolproof is to underestimate the ingenuity of complete fools.
**Douglas Adams**

## Speed

In this competitive and fast-moving world, it's easy for your idea to become outdated and no longer relevant, or for your competitors's products to be launched first. Speed to market is vital, and constructing the brief should not delay the development process. Good teamwork skills and adopting a process of concurrent engineering are key success factors here.

### Concurrent engineering

This is the term given to a process of engaging all relevant design tasks simultaneously rather than sequentially. It is no good, for example, developing a brief if sometime later a production engineer provides alternative production methods, or if a market researcher wishes to correct some consumer information. Team working is the embodiment of concurrent engineering and incorporates issues of trust, consensual decision-making and the good use of communications technology.

# Jonathan Ive

## Biography

Born in 1967, Jonathan Ive studied art and design at what is now Northumbria University. At 22, he became a partner in London-based design consultancy Tangerine, moving three years later to join the Apple design team in California, where he has since become Senior Vice President of Industrial Design. The Apple team have released the iconic iMac, iBook, Cube, Powerbook G4, iPod and iPhone. In 2003 Jonathan Ive was recognised by the UK's Design Museum as their inaugural designer of the year.

## The iPod and the iPhone

Apple's product design specification for the iPod was to create a music device capable of storing up to 4000 songs that could be accessed via a simple and intuitive interface. Behind these simple marketing premises, however, lay a host of additional technical and legal requirements relating, for example, to trademarks, copyright, software, file storage, data transfer, interfacing, connectivity, hardware, sound characteristics and power. That Apple got these details right is demonstrated by hugely favourable industry and consumer reviews and by outstanding sales figures of over 150 million units worldwide.

Additional unique selling points were created by the iTunes downloading facility and by giving the iPod an iconic feel, which was created by a simple construction, using twin-shot polycarbonate/ABS snapped to a polished and laser-etched stainless steel back. The classic iPod also spawned a range of associated products, including the Touch, Nano and Shuffle, to meet a range of targeted consumer groups and each of these versions have been continually improved through a series of incremental developments.

**▶ iPhone by Jonathan Ive and the Apple design team**
The iPhone combines three products in one — a phone, an iPod and an Internet device.
Photograph: Apple Inc.

Having set the benchmark high with the iPod, Apple needed to again meet expectations with its mobile phone product, which was released to the US market in June 2007. The iPhone has offered features including a flush multi-touch screen with a virtually rendered keyboard, a camera, portable media player (equivalent to the iPod), text messaging functionality, visual voicemail, email, web browsing, and local Wi-Fi connectivity. The iPhone is small, easy to use and solid, but its cost and durability have been questioned. Nevertheless, Apple is near to its sales target of ten million units (which is double that of some of its competitors). The iPhone was named Time magazine's Invention of the Year in 2007, and was later upgraded to include 3G and assisted GPS.

Like the iPod, the iPhone has to satisfy vast technical and legal requirements as well as consumer requirements. Products must meet performance and safety standards in audio, visual and power functions. To meet environmental needs, for example, the iPhone restricts PVC, bromine and mercury in its production.

Ive is quick to point out that the success of these products can be attributed to teams working together, which requires good communication and clear goals. He also cites 'fanatical care beyond the obvious stuff' achieved through attention to detail in tools, materials and manufacturing. Communications, goals, regulations, speed, knowledge and assessment are not just the designer's responsibilities, however, and design-focused companies such as Apple are successful at embedding these issues into company culture as part of the core corporate strategy.

◀ **iPod** (facing page)
**and iPhone** (this page)
**by Jonathan Ive and**
**the Apple design team**
Photographs: Apple Inc.

# Chapter summary

This chapter has highlighted ways to shape the product idea into a more tangible statement, drawing on some of the consumer needs, current market trends and practical and statutory requirements. There is real skill in weaving together the key facts to create a feasible summative picture.

For some, this is based on an intuitive feel for what's new and what's right. For others, this will mean a more objective analysis based on a whole range of data including market, economic and political factors. It can also include psychological factors such as motivations, perceptions, beliefs and attitudes.

Whatever approach is preferred, it is important to get the product brief right. Get it wrong and time, money and effort will be committed to a design process that can only lead to a flawed product. Once this process begins, it can be very difficult to stop. Craft-based designers may choose to keep their brief in their head or in sketch form, but most organisations should commit the brief to paper – as not doing so is cited as one of the main reasons for product failure.

The resulting specification should outline the target that the designers must now try to meet. Meeting these targets can be expensive and much of the costs lie in development, experiments, research and manufacture. With this in mind, perhaps the specification should pose one initial question: is the project worth the expense and effort of developing at all?

### Exercise 2

Designing products often involves making things faster, better or stronger. There is, however, a school of thought that says things should be slower. For example, do you really need to make a cup of tea instantly? Do you need to stand over the kettle whilst you wait for it to boil? Imagine a kettle that slowly brings water to the boil, saving energy as it does so and letting you know when it's ready (as stove kettles used to do). Try generating the concepts behind a range of 'slow' products.

### Exercise 1

Consider which new product released to market in the past 100 years might be considered the most innovative, based on the criteria of having made the simplest change, yet having created the biggest impact on people's lives.

### Exercise 3

Produce a set of 12 criteria by which you might benchmark mobile phones. Your criteria might include, for example, the ease of pressing the buttons and using the menu, and the ability to adjust the volume. Conduct a series of tests on a range of mobile phones to consider which one might be the ultimate performer. After your benchmarking analysis, reappraise your criteria and order them according to their importance.

▲ **Cupboard by
Straight Line Designs**
Colourful and humorous
products clearly appeal to
children, but stressful and
busy lives can mean that
adults too enjoy the benefits
of playful furniture too.

# Design solutions

You see things, and you say: 'Why?'
But I dream things that never were
and I say 'Why not?'
**George Bernard Shaw**

**This chapter outlines some of
the techniques designers have at
their disposal to meet the creative
challenges set by new product ideas
and specifications. These techniques
are grouped into three different
sections. The first outlines a series
of tools that relate to how the product
will interact with people, the second
lists some of the aids to conceptual
thinking and the third provides
key aspects to consider in making
functional products.**

◀ **Morph device concept
by Nokia**

# Meeting needs

Sometimes a new product just seems to look, feel or work in such a way it makes you wonder why it wasn't done that way before. A skilled designer is one who is able to understand just what a product needs and find the ways to provide it.

Here, we look at some of the ideas and techniques that can aid this aspect of product design.

## Form and function

A common debate in product design concerns the precedence of form (i.e. aesthetic or shape) or function (i.e. its purpose). The debate centres on which to design first: a product's form or its function. For example, if you are designing a wine glass and focus on the form first, generating a fantastically evocative flute, you might end up with something that holds no liquid and can't easily be drunk from. If you focus on the function so that the glass can hold 33cl of wine then you might end up with a wine glass that looks like any other.

The principle of 'form follows function' was developed early in the twentieth century and was taken up by the Bauhaus and industrial designers such as Raymond Loewy, Henry Dreyfuss and Victor Papanek. Opponents argue that if the function is optimised, then the form becomes ubiquitous and simplified to the point where one design fits all, which could be boring or impractical.

In reality, the type of product is important in this debate, and issues such as meaning have risen to take as much prominence in thinking as form and function alone. However, it can be informative to approach a new design from these two purist perspectives.

## The Bauhaus

The Bauhaus School (1919–1933) was founded in Germany by Walter Gropius. Its rationale lay in experimentation, with influences stemming from such areas as the release of censorship generated by the former German monarch and the cultural changes being driven in Russia to theories on art, mass production and technology function.

Bauhaus philosophy therefore held little credence for tradition and the design 'style' that developed is noted for its simplicity and harmony between function and form with strong leanings towards the rationality of modernism. The ideas and subsequent fleeing of designers from Nazi Germany has meant that Bauhaus ideas have had an important worldwide influence over design thinking.

**Semantics**

An important transition in design thinking is to view a product as not simply something with a form and a function, but as something that can impart meaning to people and that might therefore be considered an artefact. A product should therefore announce what it is, what it is for and how it can be used and should also provide feedback that it is being used correctly. This might mean that fast cars should look sleek and streamlined while an off-road car should look rugged and robust, but there can be significant deeper subtleties at work beyond styling. For example, some cars have a push-button start instead of a key switch – this sort of ignition usually taking the form of a simple, black, round button. Designing a contrasting bezel frame and dished surface might indicate the 'push' requirement of the switch.

**Culture**

In exploring semantics, it's important to recognise that different individuals and societies may attach different meanings to the messages imparted. The colour black, for example, may signify cool and hip in some countries, but will indicate death and mourning in others. Designers may have to consider meaning that is optimised for a wider global audience, or consider making a range of designs to meet different cultures.

It is here that the issue of globalisation opens up a fierce debate. Is it acceptable to export an omnipresent design which ends up contributing to a common world culture at the expense of individual local cultures and traditions? If the argument is extended further it can be asked if it is ethical to export western and northern hemisphere products *at all* at the expense of local, indigenous designers? Even well-intentioned development initiatives can be questioned against a backdrop of enhancing local design solutions rather than imposing technological new ones.

Objects do not have meaning. But if an object is thoughtful, we project meaning onto it in daily life.
**Karim Rashid**

The most exciting opportunity for innovation lies in combining the knowledge systems, tools and social and territorial assets of south and north.
**John Thackara**

◀ **This Little Piggy by Becky Miller**

This piggy bank has a pig-like form and the function of collecting money. However, its form changes – the pig gets fatter as more coins are saved – lending an emotional element to the design. How big should the pig get before it is slaughtered?

Photographs: Becky Miller

**Design and emotional satisfaction**

Consider how a car's push-button start could be redesigned to impart some element of emotional satisfaction? The Aston Martin DBS has a small, glass briquette that slides into a slot on the steel dashboard and glows deep red when the engine is ready to fire, a highly fitting function to power up a six-litre V12 luxury sports car.

## Ergonomics

Ergonomics (or human factors engineering) is the name given to the process of designing according to human needs in order to optimise well-being and overall system performance. Traditionally this has referred to ease of use and physical fit between a product and its user based on anthropometrical data. For example, making the diameter of a handgrip a size that fits comfortably for a defined range of the population.

However, more modern perspectives include cognitive ergonomics, which covers aspects of aesthetics, expectation, perception and sensory satisfaction. Taking these factors into account, our example of a cylindrical handgrip might be the right diameter, but cognitive ergonomics mean that there is now a user expectation as to what it feels like to touch and grip and how it moves and works to take into account. A warm, shape-changing foam rubber coating might provide a more satisfactory experience than a straightforward metal tube.

## Affective design

Affective design is a branch of ergonomic thinking that is concerned with the emotional effect that a product has on a user based on their interaction with it. It is the way that a product 'affects' a person resulting in an emotional or behavioural response, which can add significant depth to a design. The aim is to deliver products that, for example, delight.

Consider a table lamp that adjusts its own level of brightness to the ambient light level. The form and function remain the same as a standard table lamp, as too will the ergonomic action of switching it on, but there may be an emotional pleasure to be derived from having a uniform lux level whilst reading or knowing that energy consumption is being optimised. Affective design draws on scientific methods rather than the designer's intuition alone.

Emotions can, however, be fickle or transient, leading to products where attributes soon fade. Emotionally Durable Design links the principles of affective design with sustainability. If a person has a strong enough emotional attachment to a product then they are less likely to throw it away.

### Problem analysis

It is often tempting to try and conjure up a good idea or a design solution from nowhere, but this isn't always an easy thing to do. You could spend weeks trying to come up with a good idea for a car and at best create something fairly obvious. It can be easier if you start by identifying the problems. With a car, for example, this might include the fact that opening a car window often leads to thumping air pressure changes, wind noise, drafts and rain. If there are many problems identified then it can be helpful to rank these in order of importance so that the key areas can be tackled first. This might be done by multiplying the likelihood of the problem occurring by the impact the problem has when it occurs.

A Failure Mode and Effect Analysis (FMEA) is a matrix that not only identifies potential failures in design and manufacturing, but includes columns to show what changes are suggested. This visual and collated chart is often used later in the process to check designs. FMEAs are equally as valid as problem analysis techniques and, in this context, as creative tools.

### Scenario analysis

Trying to generate new ideas for a product now can be aided if you know where the product is heading by locating the concept in a future setting. For example, what will people want from your product in ten years' time, and could you work towards delivering these wants now? Are there any links or common issues across the range of scenarios? Are there any seed trends (current trends that might develop in future)? Are there any parallel scenarios or precursor trends (ones that are based on similar or previous behaviours)? Thinking through several scenarios with a panel of people with mixed backgrounds is ideal.

Design is a plan for arranging elements in such a way as best to accomplish a particular purpose.
**Charles Eames**

### ► Morph device concept by Nokia

The Nokia Morph is a concept which demonstrates the functionality that nanotechnology might be capable of delivering, including, for example, flexible materials, transparent electronics, self-cleaning surfaces and the ability to harvest its own energy.

I don't have any furniture of
mine in my room.
**Marc Newson**

### Analogy

Drawing an analogy is to make a comparison between things and is a feature behind many approaches to creativity. For example, an airplane is analogous to a bird in that both can fly, have wings, can travel for a long way without landing and sense where they are going. They are dissimilar in that they fly through different means and work in different ways. Therefore, if your specification is related to the development of airplane wings, is there a solution that can be derived from birds?

Analogies can be natural, personal, remote or fantastical and are often just used very informally: 'this problem makes me think of X (analogy) – that suggests to me that maybe we could try Y (idea drawn from analogy X)'.

### Bionics

The term 'bionics' has been used to describe the systematic use of biological and botanical analogies to solve engineering and design problems. Rippled skins on warships rather than smooth hulls, for example, replicates shark skin and enables more efficient transmission through water.

## Features

The features of a design are those responses generated by the designer to meet the criteria in the product design specification. But which criteria and feature should be looked at first? Whilst the specification may identify the criteria, sometimes the criteria requirements can be contradictory and it can be overwhelming to know just where to start. Even knowing which criteria is prioritised to be the more important does not mean that it is the right criteria in the design to start with. It is the designer's role to think through the sequence of the design as far as possible in order to maximise the functional response.

Much research into design methodology revolves around answering this question of knowing just where to start. For example, the design for product 'X' involved the development of a set of guidelines about the product's criteria and, importantly, their links. Axiomatic design uses a matrix to map the key issues and a set of design principles (axioms) to facilitate the ensuing process.

## Quality

Designers must remember that they are usually designing for others and not for themselves. In product design, the term 'quality' has come to define the philosophy of meeting customer needs. For example, an expensive luxury sports car might not be a quality product if the consumer needs are to transport a family of small children to school every morning. It's good practice to remember this and to ensure that the specification is understood and not distorted by personal ambitions or perceptions.

### Quality function deployment

Quality is a philosophy but the concept also has a number of practical tools associated with it. Quality function deployment (QFD), for example, is a technique for mapping customer requirements against the features created by the designer. It is a quantifiable technique allowing the matches to be compared against a range of design solutions and scored so that the best design can be selected. It can also grade other characteristics such as technical difficulty and, because it is a visual technique, QFD is a powerful communications tool.

Quality is remembered long after the price is forgotten.
**Gucci motto**

# Droog

94

## Biography

Amsterdam-based enterprise Droog was established in 1993 by Gijs Bakker and Renny Ramakers as a collective of like-minded designers. Droog is derived from the Dutch word for 'dry' and is more about ethos than style. The collective has seen works produced by over 100 designers including Marcel Wanders, Tejo Remy and Jurgen Bey. Droog burst on the scene at the 1993 Milan Furniture Fair, challenging many of the traditional designers whose works had become more austere against the colourful, decadent design of the 1960s and 70s.

## Affective design

The collective has developed their so-called 'Droog mentality', which is a statement of product design that involves creating innovative concepts that users can immediately connect with, while simultaneously challenging their perspectives and expectations. Bakker and Ramaker consider themselves 'curators' of this ethos and have referred to Droog designers as authors that 'generate experience, interaction, participation and products that are easy to comprehend, have meaning, tell stories' [Bakker].

The stories that Droog products tell are often contradictory, counter-intuitive or humorous (incorporating a dry wit). The communication varies from the sublime to the outrageous, but the connections are always rooted in powerful contemporary societal issues such the pace of life, the need for individuality or memories and nostalgia. This makes it possible for seemingly simple and trivial products to be capable of making quite profound statements. Such affective design is an important element in lifting a product to meet people's needs beyond mere form and function. Droog products cannot always be said to be practical, or feasible beyond prototyping, but they do illustrate the powers that designers have when raising questions about culture, semiotics, problems and consumerism.

▲ **Tablecloth with bowl by
Saar Oosterhof/Droog**
Photograph:
Marsel Loermans

◄ **Powerpoint by
Peter Hopman/Droog**
Powerpoint forms part
of Droog's project on
'The Inevitable Ornament',
which explores the
uncertainty of rules
surrounding ornamentation.
The Powerpoint light (and
tablecloth with bowl, featured
above) aim to illustrate
and question whether or
not technology can be its
own decoration.
Photograph:
Feddow Claassen

## ▶ Shaving set of razor and brush by Dick van Hoff/Droog

There are hundreds of shaving brushes available, made from different materials and featuring different colours and different shaped handles, but virtually all have exactly the same form: a set of bristles held at one end by a small pot. This design is simple but unique in its conception, obvious in hindsight, and clear in its function.

Photograph:
Thea van den Heuval

◀ **Function Tiles** (top left and above) **and Towel Hook** (bottom left) **by Peter van der Jagt, Erik-Jan Kwakkel, Arnout Visser/Droog**
A series of products that question whether a wall tile has to simply be wall tile. Hooks, cubes, bulges, cupboards and drawers, are among the ideas explored in Droog's Functional Tiles range.
Photographs: E. Moritz

# Concept development

This section looks at some of the aids that assist conceptual thinking. These aids are effectively the tools of the trade that designers can use to help with the cerebral process of design. An ability to get ideas down into some pictorial representation is fundamental in clarifying and testing thoughts, providing new perspectives and committing ideas to permanent record. This process of 'externalising' means you don't actually have to be good at art, but the clearer you can make your visuals the more clarity you can provide and the more credibility you will have in discussing ideas with others.

## Visualisation

Sketching is a good way to help visualise form. Most sketches may be simple pencil line drawings, and this is often all that's needed to develop ideas further. It's easy, however, to find simple techniques that can create a more professional appearance. Line strengths can be varied to highlight outlines, simple shading can lift a sketch off the page and provide three-dimensional depth and marker pens can be used to embellish colour and lighting. Projections are different ways to present a three-dimensional object in two-dimensional form.

Lines that appear parallel but actually converge onto a distant point can also provide depth to a drawing. This form of perspective drawing is referred to as iconic projection and it provides a greater sense of reality to line art that has an oblique or isometric projection. An orthographic projection displays a three-dimensional product in a two-dimensional way through its top (plan), front and side views. It is used in manufacturing but can have a role to play in helping to map out the basic features behind a product at the concept stage.

## Computer-aided design

The use of computers for visual communication requires different perceptive skills to those used in drawing. Freehand drawing requires hand and eye co-ordination along with an individual style – usually left to right and working backwards or forwards. A computer-drawn image works in planes and layers and requires less co-ordination and style, but calls on more spatial awareness and levels of abstraction.

There is a distinction to be made between software that is intended to aid drawing and sketching and software designed for more engineering-based applications (although the distinction in some cases is becoming less clear). Solid modelling in some computer-aided design (CAD) packages allows the design intent to be sketched in engineering packages with relative ease.

Beware, though: CAD drawings can be visually impressive so designers can get hooked into using CAD and therefore locked into design forms when sketching would be a more appropriate course of action.

### ▶ Segway development

CAD drawings offer an advantage because they can perform a number of functions, from computing volumes or listing parts to calculating stresses and mould flows. In particular, they can be 'unwrapped' into orthographic projections or exploded, as is the case here, to provide essential manufacturing information.

Photograph: segway.com

### File formats

The ability to save images in appropriate formats is important. Usual formats for graphics applications include JPEG, TIFF, BMP or PNP. A tagged image file format (TIFF) is often the preferred format for professional reports and flyers because of the flexibility and simplicity it caters for in compression and instruction. For more engineering-based packages, file formats include IGES, STEP, DXF and DRG. It is important to consider the right format in order to be able to exchange CAD data with client or manufacturing partners.

### ▼ Deena Low Table for Habitat

A sketch can help to visualise complex three-dimensional forms such as this structural coffee table made from an array of colour-lacquered, slatted beech plywood.

Case study: Droog ▼ Concept development ▼ Case study: Josef Cadek

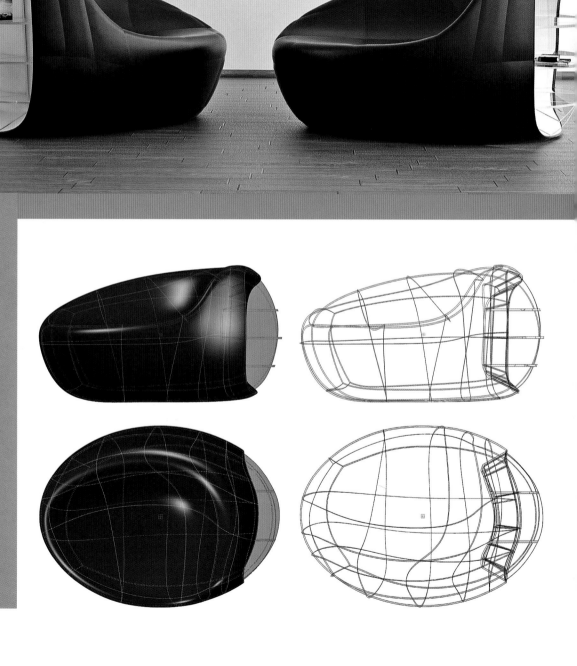

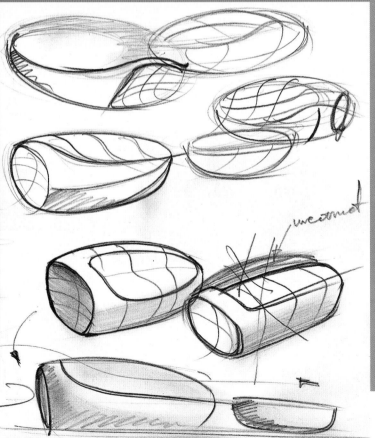

◀ **ZernO by
man>works> design**
Sit? Lounge? Recline?
Talk? Watch? The ZernO
explores and offers ideas
for the way that people and
sofas interact.

## Modelling

The creation of models is a vital tool in providing the true feel of a concept. Models can be symbolic (such as a mathematical equation) or physical. In the study of design, and especially when undertaking a design course, the development and use of models is inevitable, but what they're actually for is often lost in the pressure to create excellence. A very beautiful and detailed physical model can elicit much praise, but may well be totally inappropriate to the stage of design. There can also be a strong desire to explore every stage in the design with a costly model. It is therefore very important to be able to select the most appropriate and cost-effective model to suit the stage of the design that is being undertaken and not to waste your precious resources on a model that will do little to aid the final design. A simple white card model can be just as instructive as a fully-built prototype.

First and foremost a model should be created to help predict the future of an idea. This can help to shape the thinking behind the appearance, performance and expectations of a design. Communicating a design idea to others is a secondary function.

## Symbolic models

One of the most effective and cheapest ways of generating a working design is by using mathematical models that give an understanding of a function or system. The model need not be complex; for example:

$$force = mass \times acceleration$$

might be used to model a child's foot standing on a scooter, but a few minutes of calculation can save many hours and wasted effort with more elaborate approaches or experiment building. Mathematical models can be used to locate pivot points, to calculate sizes and outputs or to predict how designs will behave when variables such as force or temperature are changed. However, it is important to keep in mind that these models are only symbolic representations of reality and answers should be treated as informative rather than exact.

### ▶ Decanter No.2 by Etienne Meneau

This is a limited edition wine decanter by Etienne Meneau. Product designers can look towards the attention in function and form that sculptors such as Meneau bring to the development process.

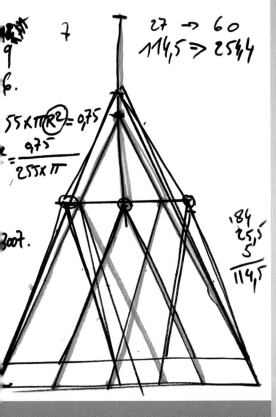

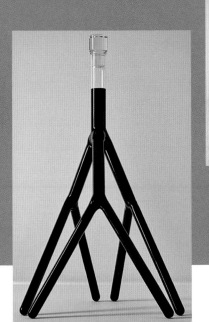

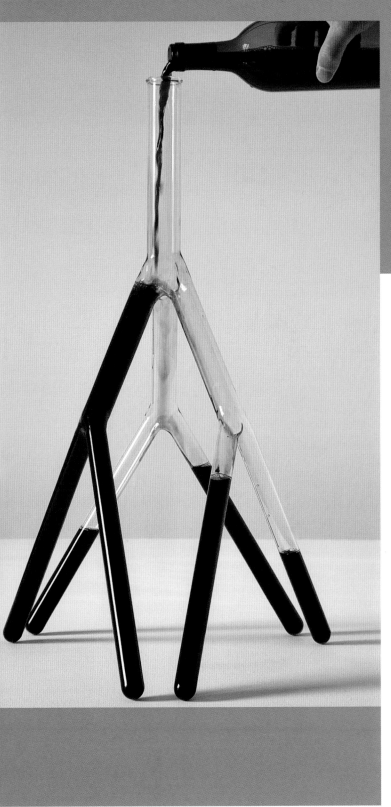

### ▶ Aluminium bottles by Sigg

Sigg water bottles are made from a single piece of aluminium that is impact extruded. This means they can be lightweight, but avoid having a seam so ensuring a constant aesthetic and durability. The inside is hygienically coated to help alleviate contamination of contents.

### ▶ Hotpaper toaster by Olivier Gregoire

There might be a range of areas to explore in the design of a toaster including, for example, ways of toasting bread, controlling the function of retrieving toast after it has been cooked as well as the visual aspect of the design. The Hotpaper toaster explores ideas around visualistion. Of his design, Gregoire says:

'I wanted to create something more unique by a contemporary approach of material. As for the design, I wanted something that disregarded the product itself by favouring the visual impact.'

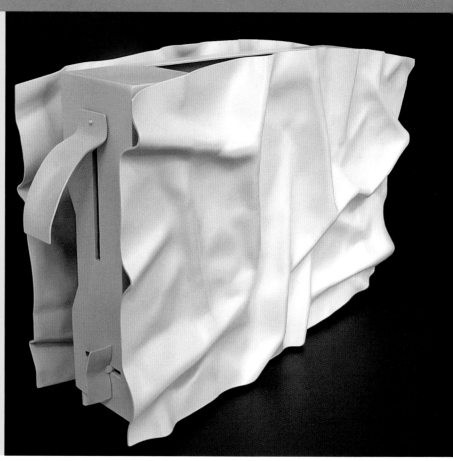

**◄ Lemon Squeezer by Tools Design**

Once an area has been identified, a good designer will explore a range of solutions. Obtaining juice directly from a fruit, for example, can be achieved in many different ways.

I tried a dozen different modifications that were rejected. But they all served as a path to the final design.
**Mikhail Kalashnikov**

## TRIZ

TRIZ is taken from the Russian phrase '*teoriya resheniya izobretatelskikh zadatch*' meaning the 'theory of inventive problem solving'. This a premise based on the study of innovation over many years that there is always a set of standard solutions to a specific problem. TRIZ therefore advocates that if a problem is described to a computer, a computer database can generate possible solutions. This is a systematic approach to generating solutions unlike, for example, the random approaches of brainstorming.

## A range of solutions

A designer who feels pleased at their ability to develop a speedy solution often has a long time to regret this early haste, and the marketplace is littered with examples of designs that could be better. Good design practice explores many ways in which an overall concept can be met by producing a wide range of solutions. A designer knows this and allows themself the necessary time and space, even when the pressure from clients to find solutions is high.

## Making choices

Time and resource restrictions mean that not all solutions generated can be taken forward and it is usual to select just one or two for further exploration. It is obviously important to make the right choice and not discard the better ideas. In fact, decisions are constantly required in design, not just in selecting a design but in how to go about appropriate research, who to research, how much to spend, where to start detailed design, which options to select and what materials to use. Good decision-making is a major but often overlooked area of design.

Often in life, the first answer is the right answer and sometimes this is true in design too. There is usually, however, scope for developing a solution into a better and better state. This iterative process of evolving the optimum design demands time and mental strength because further sketching, discussion and reflection can seem unnecessary when the idea already seems good and where there is client pressure to find solutions quickly.

106

▶ **EOS 40D by Canon**
Digital camera designers have to make decisions about a host of features. The magnesium-clad body of the EOS 40D is considered by many to house a perfectly-selected range of features, making it the leader in a highly-competitive market.

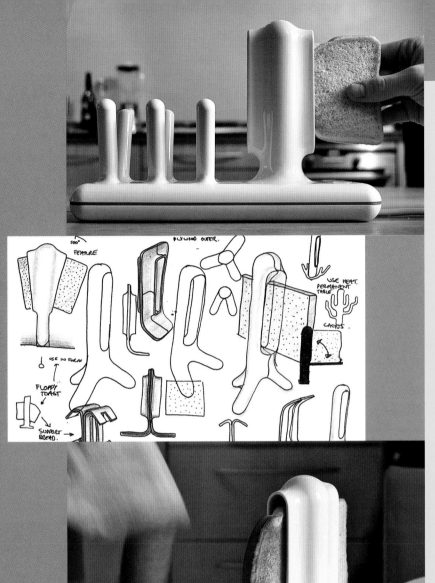

## ◄ Glide/ceramic toaster by George Watson

There has been little development of the toaster since the start of the twentieth century; whilst other appliances have developed and improved, incorporating new technologies and thinking, the toaster has remained relatively untouched. When it was first invented eating toast was a social activity that took place at the breakfast table; these days toasters have been relegated to cheap plastic objects hidden away in the kitchen. George Watson's Glide/ceramic toaster is designed to engage the user and reinvigorate the social context of breakfast.

# Josef Cadek

## Biography

Josef Cadek is a young Czech designer, born in 1980 and graduating from Prague's Technological University in 2005. His love of product design stems from 'creating something by your brain, hands, mind and soul. This "human touch" moves things you have done from just a product to creation and that is the most beautiful thing about design.'

Good designers are willing to engage and challenge both themselves and their colleagues in a quest to achieve better and better ideas. This enthusiasm for generating product concepts is seen in Cadek's willingness to engage not just with educational and work-based projects, but with a wide variety of design competitions, exhibitions and online design forums.

## The Locust bike concept

Cadek's Locust Bike is an ingenious design concept. It can be folded to a small size and so is easy to store, but because of its relatively standard-size wheels it offers cyclists the same feel and riding experience of a normal non-folding bike.

The Locust's main feature is the circular frame, which makes the unusual folding mechanism possible. Both wheels have overhung mounting. After releasing the safety-lock nuts, the wheels are turned around the relevant axis and into the frame. Because the rear wheel folds, momentum transfer from the crank set to the rear wheel must be divisible.

On the Locust, the conventional chain system found on other bikes is replaced by a belt system with outer toothing and the belt is mounted on two rollers. Both the chain wheel and the pinion have outer toothing, ensuring correct rotational direction as well as divisibility of the whole system.

The red safety lock releases the saddle support to fold the saddle down towards the frame. To fold the handlebars, the revolving safety-lock nut on the top of the head set is first released. The handlebars can then be moved back towards the frame. The Locust is equipped with a disc brake in front and a clamshell brake at rear, thus preventing blockage of the folding mechanism. The colour scheme was conceived with safety in mind.

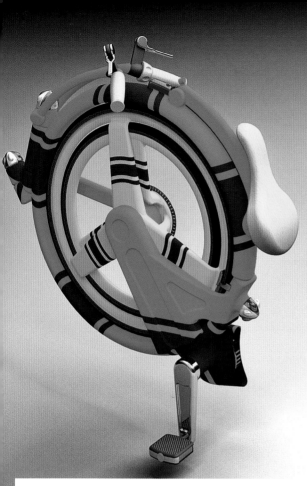

**◀ Locust folding bike by Josef Cadek**

The Locust folding bike is an example of innovation in bicycle design. Bicycle innovations form one of the biggest sectors for new patents.
Photographs:
© Josef Cadek
www.cadekdesign.com

Cadek's bike is just one of a number of innovations being seen in folding bikes, which are gaining popularity as the need to commute by public rather than personal transport becomes greater and as space becomes more imperative. It illustrates the way in which designers can stretch their imaginations and work hard to develop a range of design concepts and turn these into design solutions.

Concept development ▼ Case study: Josef Cadek ▼ Functionality

### ▶ Locust folding bike by Josef Cadek

Whilst experience can help in design practice, it's also an axiom of design that anybody can have a good idea, and young designers can particularly challenge incumbent thinking.

Many young designers incorrectly think that sketching is a means to creating a beautifully crafted image rather than a tool for generating and communicating thoughts, a process that CAD is not capable of replicating. New ideas will often develop from these doodles. The idea for the Locust bike was first conceived with drawing before moving towards these CAD visuals.

Photographs:
© Josef Cadek
www.cadekdesign.com

**Q&As**

Where did the idea for the Locust bike come from?

**Joseph Cadek**  I am not sure about this. Now when I look at the Locust bike, it seems so logical and simple that it really surprises me sometimes that I was the first one with this idea. It is so obvious … or it looks so to me now. It is almost always like that in the design process. It can be difficult and complicated to discover the simple!

What process did you use in developing the initial idea into the design that emerged?

**JC**  It is like solving an equation with an unlimited number of unknowns (note I am an engineering type of designer). It is impossible to solve these unknowns in one go, but I can just decide: 'this will look like this, this will work like that' and that reduced the number of unknowns. Slowly but surely the design gets less and less fuzzy and foggy. Meanwhile it is growing in your mind, and it is getting real.

Do you use a combination of sketching, CAD and models?

**JC**  Yes, pencil and paper are the fastest at the beginning, but then advanced 3D is crucial. I am not from a generation of designers who were able to design the most complex products using only stationery (I admire those designers and engineers very much, but I need a computer).

The Locust is just a concept bike, but the evolution, Locust Two, is now under current development. Locust Two offers improvements in practicality, weight, simplicity and overall user experience. What did you learn from Locust One that has helped you develop Locust Two?

**JC**  A lot basically everything Locust Two is based on!

# Functionality

Functionality is about bringing a product to life. This can mean making it work or move, but can also simply mean choosing the right materials to construct the form and components. Most designers like to have some idea of what different materials can be used for what different purposes. An exhaustive knowledge and experience will help, but understanding the basic properties of materials will allow a better understanding behind the selection process.

## Material properties

The most common properties that a product designer requires from materials are mechanical in nature: its hardness, strength, toughness and ductility. These have specific meanings in engineering and defined values that can be used to calculate how thick or thin a part should be to avoid failure. Most of these properties are constant, but can change according to temperature or pressure and 'fatigue failure' or 'creep' can cause failures at levels below those expected. Properties such as electrical, thermal, chemical, magnetic and optical might need to be considered for specific product functions.

## Tensile strength

The ultimate tensile strength is the maximum stress (the force applied on a specific area) that a material can withstand before it becomes irreparably damaged. Brittle materials like glass might simply reach that limit and then snap, but most materials including metals will stretch first (returning to their original shape up to a point) then deforming permanently and ultimately breaking. This pattern of behaviour can be mapped through a stress/strain diagram.

**Stress/strain diagram for steel**

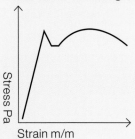

Stress Pa

Strain m/m

▶ **Umbrella Pot designed by Kouichi Okamoto, Kyouei design**

The pure white lines of this ceramic umbrella pot give it a clean, stylish and contemporary look although the material it is made from is 'Tokoname-yaki', a kind of traditional Japanese ceramic of clay and feldspar (or silica) glaze that dates back to the 1100s. Water that drains from the umbrellas placed within it help to provide a drink for the plant through internal holes inside the design.

### Metals

Each new development of metal (bronze, iron, cast iron and steel) has spurred civilisation forward. The major metals used today are iron, aluminium, copper, zinc and magnesium. These are hard, strong, dense materials that can be moulded, cut or formed into shapes.

Aluminium, for example, can be found in cars, bicycles, saucepans, watches and cans, but rarely in its pure form, as it is relatively soft. Instead it is usually alloyed with elements such as copper, zinc, magnesium manganese and silicon to form an alloy commonly known by its trade name of Duralimin. Metals can be recycled, and in the UK roughly 40% of steel is comprised of recycled metal.

### Ceramics

Ceramics are non-organic, non-metallic materials such as concrete, clay, brick and glass that can be moulded or sintered into shape. They are generally hard, porous and brittle, which makes them ideal for low volume tableware or lifestyle products or for specific applications where the electro-mechanical properties of ceramics can also be ideally suited. These properties can be enhanced with oxide and non-oxide inclusions. Titanium carbide is used, for example, in scratchproof watches and zirconium dioxide in ceramic knife blades; these are harder than steel and can stay sharper up for to ten times longer.

◀ **Wood bikes by Xylon Bikes**

By using wood as the main component of a bicycle, Xylon has attempted to redefine the nature of a bike frame itself. The perforated frame of the Cell bike, for example, draws on principles of bionic design, simulating the cellular nature of wood.

Research is what I'm doing
when I don't know what
I'm doing.
**Wernher von Braun**

**Wood**

Wood is one of our earliest design materials and it comes in a wide variety of forms, each with different properties. At the end of its working life, timber decays naturally or can be burnt to recoup heat energy. The carbon dioxide emitted is considered equal to the carbon dioxide that is absorbed during its growth process, making it a carbon-neutral material. It can be sourced locally, or from sustainable sources authenticated to replace trees as they are felled.

One of the problems with the use of timber in mass production is the presence of weaknesses such as knots and fissures, which make it impossible to guarantee its consistency or integrity. Wood-based products that work by reforming particle fibres overcome this issue and include medium density fibreboard (MDF), melamine-faced chipboard and plywood, plus an increasing number of new products including wood-plastic composites, which can be moulded, providing designers with new opportunities. The disadvantages of using these sorts of timber are the chemical nature of the glues and resins that are usually used as binders.

**Polymers**

Plastic is a term commonly used to describe synthetic oil-derived materials, but it can also describe the malleability of materials including metals. It is more correct to refer to plastics as 'polymers', which describes materials that have repeating chains of molecules in both synthetic and natural materials. There is a wide range of polymers at the designer's disposal with properties such as flexibility and colour that can be adjusted with ease and formed into complex shapes and sizes.

Drawbacks include degradation over time and difficulty in recycling for some polymers, although advances in technology are making this easier. Laser refraction, for example, is able to sort plastic bottles into types at great speed, recycled materials are increasingly available and biopolymers (ones made from plant constituents such as corn) are developing rapidly.

**New materials**

Developments are continually being made in material science. For example, Glass-Reinforced Fibre Metal Laminate (GLARE) is a material composed of very thin layers of metal such as aluminium interspersed with layers of glass-fibre bonded with an epoxy matrix. Although it is a composite with lay-up options that can be matched against stress points, it is constructed using conventional metalwork techniques, and is used, for example, in the manufacture of the Airbus A380.

Smart materials have properties that can be changed through external stimuli such as impact, stress or temperature, giving the designer unique behavioural opportunities. Shape-memory polymers, for example, can be deformed into one shape, but induced to form another through a temperature change. Chromogenic polymers change colour through an external stimulus such as light-sensitive sunglasses. Similarly, new gels and foams, including foamed metals, are now offering designers with equally exciting design solutions.

It can be hard to keep up to date with these rapid developments, but the designer must try. Journals, exhibitions, networks and technology transfer agents can help. It is important to weigh up the suitability of these materials against both cost and the risk involved in using technologies whose long-term effects may yet be unproven.

**Rapid prototyping**

Rapid prototyping is the name given to the technique of 'slicing' a computer-generated solid model and printing a hard form of each layer to build up a physical solid model. This can be done in a variety of ways including printing paper layers, printing layers of starch or polymer powder like an inkjet printer, or sintering polymer (or even metal) resins or powders using lasers. Each layer builds up in increments anywhere between 25um to 100um steps so there are some slight ridges, but these are barely detectable.

Rapid prototyping is ideal for making products that need to be visually inspected before they are developed further. Any subsequent redesign can be quick and just as instantaneous to review. Rapid prototyping also affords the designer the added benefit of being able to make parts that can be difficult to produce in other ways (such as complex or multiple parts or those without radii or taper).

In fact, the process offers designers opportunities to design new products that can, realistically, only be manufactured through rapid prototyping. This includes parts within parts, cavities with limited access, interlinked shapes, metal parts that phase change or are not homogenous, or those with wispy fill sections.

I just want things to work properly.
**James Dyson**

### Nanotechnology

This is concerned with manipulating atoms and molecules on a scale of 100 nanometers or smaller to make new materials or devices within that size range. Applications include bespoke molecules in sunscreens to block out harmful rays, small motors and fans inside electronic circuits and carbon nanotubes that have mechanical properties which are many thousand times greater than that of steel. Nanotubes are of a similar size to asbestos particles and there is a fear that these may have a similar disruptive influence on the body.

### ▶ Dyson washing machine

Dyson's washing machine has received mixed reviews and its success has not replicated that of the Dyson vacuum cleaners. It does, however, have a number of design features that represent great attention to the needs of the consumer and significant research enabled the development of an energy- and water-efficient cleaning contra rotating-drum system.

Photograph: Dyson Ltd.

**◀ Hidden.mgx vase by Dan Yeffet 'Jelly Lab' for Materialise**

The Hidden.mgx vase is made from polyamide (nylon) using selective laser sintering (SLS), a design that could realistically only be made by rapid prototyping. Yeffet defines his work as challenging limits and boundaries, working as an explorer and adventurer.

◀ **Kartell Thalya dining chair by Patrick Jouin**
A range of furniture designed by Patrick Jouin and produced in epoxy resin using stereolithographic rapid prototyping techniques.

Good design is probably
98% common sense. Above all,
an object must function well
and efficiently – and getting
that part right requires a
good deal of time and attention.
**Terence Conran**

## Movement

Functioning products with moving components can also be modelled in CAD, but are often best served by a physical model where feel and experience can optimise the design. Old toys, modelling and toy construction kits as well as broken equipment are ideal for simulating moving parts; having a box of bits to play with can build up engineering know-how and provide inspiration for future projects.

## Performance

From large multi-national companies to design students, the process of testing a newly completed design tends to falls at the back end of the project when time and delivery pressures can make performance testing an overlooked stage. Having worked hard on a design, a designer can also feel that the design is optimised and be reluctant to hear any negative comments. However, consumer comments, whether negative or positive, along with performance and (if necessary) destruction testing, are all a vital part of the design process. Designers must be able to learn from results, listen to criticism, argue a case if appropriate and accept a change if it's necessary. For some products, independent testing and certification is a compulsory requirement.

# d3o

## Biography

Richard Palmer studied for a degree in mechanical engineering and followed this with a course in design at the Royal College of Art in London. This unusual background took him originally to DuPont, then to his own innovation design consultancy. He is now is a founder and Chief Executive Officer of d3o, a company based on the south coast of England.

▲ **d3o smart material**

d3o smart material is available in a range of thicknesses, shapes and levels of shock absorbency. This variety of form has allowed the material to be used in a range of applications, from sports clothing and football design to ballet shoes and iPod covers.

◄ **d3o contour sheet material**

The contour sheet material is designed to 'densify' when flexed, providing extra absorbance, for example, when bending an elbow or knee.

▶ **d3o smart material**

## d3o

d3o is one of a new range of smart materials. Under normal conditions the molecular structure of d3o is loose with weak molecular bonds giving the material a soft, flexible and fluid nature. When it is hit, however, the molecules lock together to momentarily form a more rigid material. During this locking process energy is absorbed and dissipated rather than transmitted back out of the material. It may release half as much impact energy as EVA (ethyl vinyl acetate), another material with a high reputation for shock absorbance.

This locking process takes place in less than a 1,000th of a second and the faster the impact, the faster the molecules react. This type of smart material is referred to as a 'dilatant' material, meaning that its viscosity increases with the rate of shear (also referred to as non-Newtonian or a shear thickening fluid). In spite of its capabilities, d3o remains lightweight throughout the transformation and this combination of properties makes it ideal for a wide variety of protective applications such as keeping high-value goods (such as iPods) safe, or as protective clothing and equipment for stunt work and urban safety, or sports such as skiing, mountaineering or biking.

The company does not usually design products directly but works with companies that do. Even, and perhaps especially, with revolutionary innovations it can require good presentation skills and examples to persuade partners to try something new. Richard notes that, 'Sometimes it's hard to convince people what a truly amazing innovation this is until you demonstrate it. I was wearing a prototype shirt incorporating d3o, and at one point I stood up and slammed my elbow onto the table as hard as I could, sending coffee cups flying. Once they saw me doing that – without flinching – they understood what I was saying.'

Once companies buy in, the resulting products are a good example of teamwork in action. Richard is keen to stress the importance of analytical and creative backgrounds in the generation of concepts, both in his own background as well as that of his design team. Where possible, the company also ensures that the vivid orange colour of its d3o material is visible in the design so that its trademark brand becomes more and more embedded in the world of high-performance products.

# Chapter summary

This chapter has identified some of the ideas and techniques that lie behind the process of breathing life into products. The range of subjects covered has been wide. Some are more commonly used than others, but they can all be dipped into and applied as necessary.

Some of the concepts presented are also unique to design, whilst others are generic. For example, problem-solving, visualisation, presenting and knowing that there is always more than one answer to a problem are all techniques that can help in everyday life. The broad range of skills in design is increasingly recognised as useful in many aspects of business too.

To apply the ideas explored in this chapter, a wide variety of capabilities are required, such as creative, analytical, visual, spatial, technical research and skills it's not always easy to apply these techniques. Perhaps the most important requirement of all is the drive and energy needed to keep going when it would be easy to accept the current or simple answer. Thomas Edison, one of the world's greatest inventors, suggested that ideas are easy in comparison to making things work. He famously stated that success is 1 per cent inspiration and 99 per cent perspiration. And so it is.

### Exercise 1

Mobile phones have moved through distinct changes: large analogue, small analogue, large digital, small digital, hinged digital, twin hinge, folding and sliding. Use scenario analysis to consider what the design of a mobile phone might be in ten years' time. Similarly, what might be the analogous development of the portable vacuum cleaner device?

### Exercise 2

Your specification is to design a toaster. Consider and sketch 20 different ways to make toast other than with a conventional thin-wire electric toaster.

### Exercise 3

Redesign an existing wheelbarrow so that it includes:
- greater semiotic functionality
- an element of affectation.

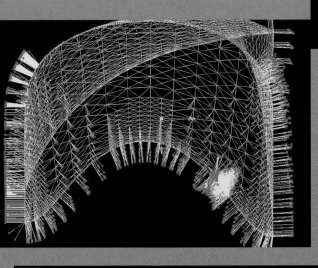

◀ **AI Stool.mgx for Materlise.mgx by Assa Ashuach**

The AI Stool was 'grown' in free space emulating the biological structure and mechanism of human bone from a DNA code using programming techniques developed by Assuach. The code optimises both for strength and aesthetic.

The usual process of product optimisation might be to calculate stresses and strains first and to refine and shape the design afterwards, but the Osteon chair works this process in reverse.

Computer code was used to determine the best internal structure needed to support the chair's required and finalised surface form; this structure was then printed out by laser sintering. It is estimated to use one-third of the material that might conventionally have been used.

Case study: d3o ▼ Chapter summary

# Production

The past is not dead, it is living in us and will be alive in the future, which we are now helping to make.
**William Morris**

**Manufacturing often seems less glamorous for designers to consider, preferring perhaps to leave this area to production engineers. It is, however, a fundamental area for consideration. A product that uses slower methods, more materials, or takes longer to assemble by just slightly more than its rivals is already at a major competitive disadvantage no matter how well it has been designed. Designers must therefore understand and work with manufacturing technologies and systems to ensure that their products are easy to make. Designers can at the same time learn and push the boundaries of manufacturing as a route to innovating new products. There is a further consideration, too. The global nature of manufacturing raises issues about society and the health of our planet that designers cannot simply ignore.**

◀ **Quin.mgx pendant lamp by Bathsheba Grossman**

# Development

The process of generating product ideas and developing concepts can be relatively cheap compared to the process of developing final manufactured products. A product that looks simple on paper can require millions of pounds' worth of investment in research, machinery, assembling, storing, testing, marketing and roll-out – and all with no guarantee of a product's success; it's hardly surprising that companies and financiers are often unwilling to take the investment risk. This is one of the biggest barriers that designers face in getting their products to market. Four key issues are highlighted here that designers should understand in helping to ensure the successful development of a production model: tolerancing, value analysis, eco-benchmarking and costing.

Be a yardstick of quality. Some people aren't used to an environment where excellence is expected.
**Steve Jobs**

## Tolerancing

The key principle behind modern mass production is that any component parts of a product should be interchangeable. There is no need to match and mate individual parts in order to make things work, and parts can be selected at random from a manufacturing process in the knowledge that they will fit together. Some of the earliest examples of this were the sheave blocks (pulleys) made for the British Navy. Marc Isambard Brunel (father of Isambard Kingdom Brunel) and Sir Samuel Bentham developed a system of simple production operations that allowed over 100,000 blocks to be made per year. The system was not widely copied in the UK, but was taken up in the US and popularised by the automobile production of Henry Ford.

To enable interchangeable fits, component dimensions have to be specified. The degree of accuracy described and the allowances made for variations in the dimensions that will still allow parts to fit together are referred to as the tolerances. Generally, the tighter and more exact the tolerances are then the more likely the fit will always work, but the more expensive it will be to produce with profound effects on costs and therefore product sales. Tolerancing products and components is therefore a balancing act between performance and production.

### ◀ Mini

BMW's new Mini design has captured much of the original Mini's iconic styling, but greater attention to production and costing details should ensure a greater profit margin than the original design offered.

### ◀ Bathtub Couch by Max McMurdo for Reestore

Eco-benchmarking a product is important, even after the end of its working life. Recycling generally refers to reusing the same material for the same purpose, such as using a milk bottle again to sell another pint of milk. It can also mean treating the material so that it can be used for other purposes. In this example, a cast-iron bath has been reused and turned into a sofa.

Development ▼ Case study: Tom Dixon

## Value analysis

A good designer should constantly seek to optimise a design throughout the development of a product. This might be an ad hoc process, looking through the different elements of each design or skimming over from one area to another. It can be done quickly by a designer (if the priority is function rather than costs) or without clarity if there are many issues being considered at the same time.

Value analysis (or value engineering) is a systematic process of assessing a design to see if improving the product's key functions can increase its value or if removing unnecessary features and functions can reduce the costs. It does this by looking at the design holistically rather than in parts and working with concepts of scoring value and cost. In this way it can reduce the amount of waste and materials used, lower costs and improve profit margins, and is therefore an important tool in creating commercially successful, mass-produced products. It often forms a part of a company's process of continuing improvement and, in some cases (in the US for example), is a requirement by law.

## Eco-benchmarking

Although the environment is of growing and serious concern to people, this may not be discernable by looking at the range and nature of products on display in the shops around you.

There are many reasons why there seems to be a slow take-up of more environmentally friendly products, including the failure to translate consumer concern into consumer demand. Designers also have to juggle with issues of a product's functions, performance, cost and safety and to make the product green adds another level of complexity. If there are no immediate economic benefits then environmental concerns can easily slip down the list of design priorities. There can also be confusion over how the designer should respond. Sometimes good intentions can actually make products more damaging to the environment. A designer who reduces the material content of a design to save resources might also end up producing a product that just breaks easily and so turns into waste more quickly.

Eco-benchmarking identifies which area(s) of a product has a high environmental effect, enabling an overall reduction in environmental impact. It also allows designers to understand and compare the environmental consequences of different design decisions. For example, benchmarking a product made of wood against one made of metal might encourage the designer to use timber because of its lower carbon dioxide emissions during processing.

## Kaizen

'Kaizen' comes from the Japanese word for improvement and its use today is concerned with the continuous improvement of a company's operation. Kaizen involves a range of issues, from waste reduction to standardisation, and its methods include individual responsibility, trust and communication. This is a different philosophical approach to more traditional authoritative business control.

Furniture manufacturing in plastics requires very costly machinery, which the Danish market is not big enough to justify. Or so they say. But show me a plastics manufacturer who dares to take on the experiment.

**Arne Jacobsen**

### Direct and indirect costs

All costing methods normally involve calculating a combination of direct and indirect costs. Direct costs are those that vary directly with the number of units sold. This typically includes the amount of time that is spent by people making one unit of product (labour cost) and the cost of material for each unit (material cost).

A product should also include an allowance to pay for costs that must be paid even if you make nothing at all (the overheads) and which do not therefore vary with the number of units sold. These are referred to as indirect costs. Indirect costs includes items such as rent, salaries, equipment, heating and lighting.

### Costing

It is vital to have an idea of the development and production costs of a new product, as well as the anticipated market size and financial gain. If the expected costs are high and the return is too low then it would be safer and easier to avoid the development risks and put the investment money into a savings account instead. Costing can be a contentious issue though. Too much heed to cost at the wrong time can stifle imagination and development, and not enough might result in overblown development costs, overpriced products and even bankruptcy. It's important therefore to have appropriate financial management systems and accurate costing methods. Amongst the costing methods are three principle techniques referred to as fixed overhead absorption rate costing (FOAR), marginal (or contribution) costing and activity-based costing (ABC).

Development ▼ Case study: Tom Dixon

# Tom Dixon

### Biography

Tom Dixon describes himself as 'a self-educated maverick whose only qualification is a one-day course in plastic bumper repair'. His early life saw him experience a variety of different cultures and his early creative works are marked by a personal interest in welding, which allowed him to create structures quickly from scrap (one of which led to his collaboration with Italian furniture company Cappellini and the realisation of the celebrated 'S' chair).

Dixon prefers to be considered an industrialist, yet he is regarded as a highly creative designer by most and has many product awards to his name. He has also been scathing towards British manufacturing and design bodies for not supporting British design and innovation sufficiently. He attempted to resolve this by setting up his own British company, Eurolounge.

### Habitat

Dixon's experience with both Cappellini and Eurolounge represented a journey away from the realm of a jobbing industrialist creator to that of a more business-savvy designer. This direction went a step further when he accepted the role of Head of Design in the UK for international home furnishing retailer Habitat.

Placing a maverick into a mainstream, corporate, retail-driven business was a risky strategy for both Habitat and Dixon. Dixon, however, was pleased to learn more about mass production, manufacturing and costing and to have access to a worldwide basket of design possibilities. In fact, he has described his decision to learn more about developing commercial products as a state of 'growing up'.

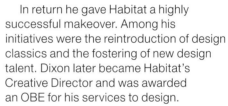

◀ **Blow Light** (facing page)**; Slab Chair** (this page, top) **and Fresh Fat Easy Chair** (this page, bottom) **all by Tom Dixon**
Photographs: Tom Dixon

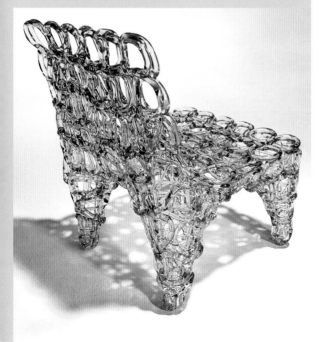

In return he gave Habitat a highly successful makeover. Among his initiatives were the reintroduction of design classics and the fostering of new design talent. Dixon later became Habitat's Creative Director and was awarded an OBE for his services to design.

Dixon has not compromised his individuality in order to be commercially successful. He continues to be innovative, creative and controversial, yet can design successfully for both the high end and the mainstream markets. He has a continuing thirst for knowledge too; ask about his current work, and he talks not just about design, ideas and creation, but about his interest in engineering, marketing, manufacturing processes and digital production.

Development ▼ Case study: Tom Dixon ▼ Manufacturing

# Manufacturing

Broadly, there are four ways to manufacture products: extracting material from solid lumps to the required shape (machining), sticking bits together to get the desired shape (fabricating), pouring non-solid materials into shape (moulding) or forcing solid materials into shape (forming).

For some, design is about experimenting, perfecting and crafting these techniques. For others, the techniques are pivotal in the large-scale production of their ideas. This section looks at these manufacturing processes with suggestions as to how they influence design thinking.

### Machining

Chipping flakes from a solid stone mass is a production technique that dates back to the creation of man's earliest products, such as axes and knives. Today's material removal is more likely to be achieved via lathes, milling machines, drills and grinders. These are flexible and accurate processes that can produce complex forms, particularly when used in conjunction with computer numerical control (CNC).

CNC can be programmed directly from a design via computer-aided manufacturing (CAM) or from parametric programming. They can be set up so that they are self-monitoring with autofeed and autotool changes, allowing the process to run overnight in lights-out factories and without operators. For the purposes of mass production, however, machining tends to be considered a slow option and the offcuts and swarf produced also make it a wasteful and therefore expensive process.

### New techniques

Advances are frequently being made in manufacturing techniques and technology. Imagine being able to grow metal forms from a single crystal, using bio-material to grow plastic parts, or using artificial intelligence to let machines monitor their own quality. In fact, some of these experimental techniques are used today, but are normally suited to small-scale or specific applications. They may, however, develop into the common techniques of the future. Whilst new developments create opportunities, many environmentalists and designers suggest that more traditional craft manufacturing techniques offer a more satisfying activity and a more sustainable future.

**Fabricating**

Fabrication describes production via the assembly of different parts, and a designer electing this form of manufacture has an array of processes at his or her disposal, such as clip-fitting, screwing, welding and gluing. Each process has its advantages and disadvantages.

Glue, for example, offers distinct advantages because it can be quickly applied and provides waterproof seals and invisible joints that have an even spread of load around the area of the seal. Glues have also benefited from advances in material science and the range of traditional natural and synthetic adhesives has been expanded with the development of drying, contact, thermoplastic, reactive, pressure-sensitive and light-curing adhesives. All of this gives the designer a much wider range of options, and products such as bicycle frames and even aeroplanes, which might have been welded in the past, can now be glued together.

However, gluing can be toxic, subject to environmental degradation and can make recycling more difficult; these factors may prompt designers to look towards the other fabrication processes. Clip-fitting or screws are generally more environmentally friendly because they allow products to be easily taken apart and reused or recycled at the end of their working life.

**Rapid manufacturing (RM)**

Rapid prototyping (RP) is used for the fast creation of models and prototypes. However, the same CAD drawings and modelling process used in RP can also be used to make the dies and moulds that are needed to produce the final manufactured products. The rapid prototyped model can actually be made in materials that are, or are close to, those specified for the final design. As such, final products rather than prototypes can even be produced using rapid prototyping techniques and this process is referred to as 'rapid manufacture' (RM).

The technique is limited by the size of parts that rapid prototyping machines can produce (roughly a maximum of 300mm cubed) and by the speed of the machines, which can be slow compared to traditional manufacturing techniques. At present, rapid manufacturing is therefore mostly limited to aerospace and medical production, but it is finding an increasing role in small batch production. As technology advances it is likely to become one of the principle manufacturing techniques of the future.

I am still mainly motivated by materials and processes but these preoccupations evolve. I am currently exploring blow moulding, vacuum metalising and computer-controlled manufacturing systems.
**Tom Dixon**

### Moulding

Moulding processes shape a pliable material into the form of a mould or die. These processes include sand-casting, die-casting, investment-casting, powder metallurgy (sintering), injection moulding, compression moulding, blow moulding, rotational moulding and vacuum-forming. In each case, the material is usually in liquid, pellet or powder form and is cast by gravity or under pressure into metal dies or into wax-, ceramic- or sand-formed cavities. Each process varies widely in the size, quality, cost, accuracy and material that can be cast so the process needs to be carefully matched against the design criteria.

Injection moulding is one of the most popular manufacturing processes among designers because it is relatively cheap and can make small or large items with reasonable accuracy. Reaction injection moulding (RIM) is a similar process except that a combination of component materials are used which have a chemical reaction within the mould itself. A typical result might be a rigid shell material with a rigid foam type internal structure, which gives a product such as a car bumper good lightness and strength.

### Forming

Forming is the shaping of a hot or cold solid material. It includes traditional blacksmithing and forge work as well as more industrialised processes such as rolling, extruding, high-energy rate forming, pressing, stamping and drop-forging. When large numbers of a product need to be made, forming is an easily automated, high-speed process involving little preparation and waste, making it ideal for mass production. Nails, crankshafts, car body panels, hinges, fire extinguishers, drink cans and cutlery are all examples of products that are made by forming processes.

Forming offers distinct advantages to the designer. Up to 160mN of force can be applied in the transformation process and accurate parts can be produced in thinner sections than can be achieved by casting. Whereas molecules in a moulding process are arranged in random patterns, forming processes offer the designer some scope for aligning the molecular grain into specific directions, providing the option to build strength in key areas. For example, railway lines are traditionally made by passing lengths of hot metal between rollers. They are then laid with a gap between them on the railway track so they do not buckle as the metal expands in the heat of the sun. Forming the lines so that the molecular structure goes across its width line and not down its length, however, means the track will expand safely in an up-and-down or sideways direction without buckling down the length of the track (and providing a smoother and quieter journey for passengers).

### ▶ Bell Sweep helmet

This helmet features a low-weight, well-ventilated design and is made using an in-mould microshell and bottom wrapped with an internal reinforcing skeleton.

### ▶ Zanzibar Tower ZTR (left) and Hot Spring (right) radiators by Bisque

Bisque radiators Hot Spring (by Paul Priestman) and Zanzibar (by Talin Dori) push the boundaries of manufacturing in steel using round and square chrome tubes to create innovative bathroom heaters.

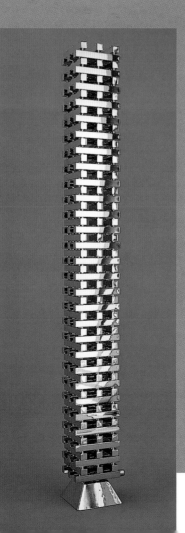

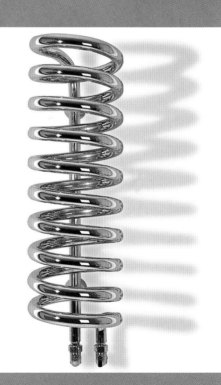

Case study: Tom Dixon ▼ Manufacturing ▼ Case study: Assa Ashuach

### ▶ Freedom of Creation 610 Lamp by Jiri Evenhuis and Janne Kyttänen

These lamp designs feature advanced materials such as Keronite and laser-sintered polyamide, combined with inspirational thinking based on natural mathematical series (such as Fibonacci). The company's products are stored digitally and can be downloaded for viewing in virtual reality environments or for production using rapid manufacturing techniques.

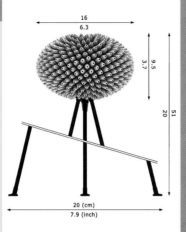

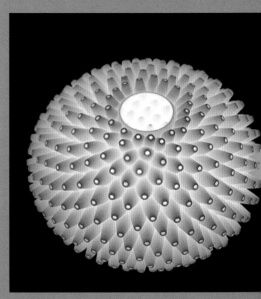

### ▶ Little Tikes Cozy Coupe® Car

Toy design has often led the way in exploring simple, safe and quick assembly techniques. The Little Tikes Cozy Coupe® Car is a children's favourite, capable of withstanding punishing treatment yet simple in its design and assembly.

**▲ Door handle by Dieter Rams**
Matt, brushed, nickel-plated and clear-laquered door furniture. Simple lines, radii and curves combine elegant styling with ease of manufacturing in this design.

## DFM and DFA

Selecting an appropriate manufacturing technique is a key task, and the designer must ensure that it and the design are well matched. If selecting a machining process, for example, the designer might choose a softer material that is easier to machine or they may provide a flat rather than a sloping surface to make it easier to drill holes. Or if moulding, they might provide sloping sides and rounded edges to help extract a molten part from a mould once it has cooled.

These design features might not be directly detailed in the product specification, but they are vital in getting a product manufactured at the lowest possible cost. These considerations should be made at an early stage in the design process, rather than finding out at the manufacturing stage that something cannot be made easily, or even at all! This consideration process is referred to as 'design for manufacture' (DFM).

The process of changing a product so that it can be put together more easily is referred to as 'design for assembly' (DFA). It is every bit as important as DFM since much of the production cost might actually be accrued at the time-intensive assembly stage. Considerations might include providing lifting lugs for heavy parts, holding points to keep it still, symmetry to make parts easier to pick up or using a standard range of bolt sizes rather than a mix of shapes and sizes. The Sony Walkman and Swatch watches are good examples of products that are designed for assembly.

# Assa Ashuach

## Biography

Assa Ashuach was born in Israel, in 1969 and since childhood he has loved to make seemingly impossible things from bits of scrap. After studying industrial design at the Bezalel Academy in Jerusalem and at London's Royal College of Art, his attention moved from bizarre scrap to more high-tech forms of manufacture.

For Ashuach, design is not just about form, function or emotion, it is about challenging and modifying traditions based on modern technologies. Now based in London, his new furniture and lights were featured at the London Design Museum, the London Design Festival and Frieze Art Fair 2005/6. Assa received the Design Museum and Esmée Fairbairn Foundation Award and the 'red dot' award for product design 2006.

Another characteristic of his work is collaborations with groups such as Materialise and ComplexMatters in the development of a new approach to materials in design.

## The Omi.mgx

One characteristic of Ashuach's work is his use of computer programmes (rather than straightforward CAD models) to instruct rapid prototyping machines. The computer programmes are a form of artificial intelligence, programmed to maximise the aesthetic and optimise the strength-to-weight ratio. It is a process that he likens to a growing process enabled by a DNA code. Ashuach refers to this as 'digital forming®' and in 2004 he created a company that develops products based on these principles.

It's not just that the thinking behind his ideas is clever, but the products that emerge are usually exquisite and seductive. The Omi.mgx light is one such example. Produced entirely as a single nylon part, its form, together with the natural flexibility of the polyamide, creates the impression of a biological mechanism. Bending or twisting the structure can transform the light's shape: twist one end and the rest will follow. This behaviour offers versatility in that it can be personalised and manipulated easily to create different sculptural sensations, space and moods.

**Q&As**

How did you first become aware of
and interested in design?

**Assa Ashuach** I was born and grew up
in a kibbutz in Israel on the Mediterranean
coast. Growing up in a kibbutz in the early
1970s was the best environment for a child
to create and play with the exciting old
machinery and exotic scraps. Visiting the
carpenter, metal workers, car mechanics
and the shoemaker, I would always end up
with great collections of bits and pieces.
I used to ask my friends to tell me their
greatest material fantasies, so I could have
the pleasure of cracking and inventing
another impossible thing.

How important is experimentation
with technology to your work?

**AA** Complex technology helps
to simplify design. Alias Studio tools
(3D software) gave us the right tools to
restrain and simplify a five-metre-long line.
SLS technology helps us to avoid elements
that are unnecessary for the design, but
are essential when production is done
with plastic injection. The Upica sofa is
a composition of four lines that creates
one compound surface. It is a very slim
and large surface that supports itself. If a
few millimetres of the surface tight shape
were changed, the sofa would collapse
like paper.

How did the Omi light project and
your relationship with Materialise
come about?

**AA** In 1999 I designed the first Omi
lamp made from 120 disposable foam
plates. The 120 plates were attached with
a rubber band, which allowed the whole
bunch to move and to create a type of
biological worm mechanism. I showed
this lamp at Salone Satellite in Milan 2000.
It got very good reactions, but was very
difficult to produce in conventional ways.
The first meeting with Naomi Kaempfer,
art director of Materialise, was just after
my RCA graduation. My experience with
3D and RP technologies together with
Materialise.mgx, a young experimental
brand, was the perfect match.

The first project we worked on was Omi.
mgx. It was to take the impossible design
into production in the only possible way.

◀ **Omi.mgx lamp**

The Omi.mgx light is one of the first products to be made immediately available to consumers as the output of an SLS (selective laser sintering) process. The lamp is made as a single nylon part with flexibility that allows it to be twisted and bent like an amorphic mutation, creating different shapes and moods. Later work, such as Ashuach's AI Light, also includes sensors that enable the light to morph itself as it hangs in space, reacting to purposeful or natural changes in light, sound or movement.

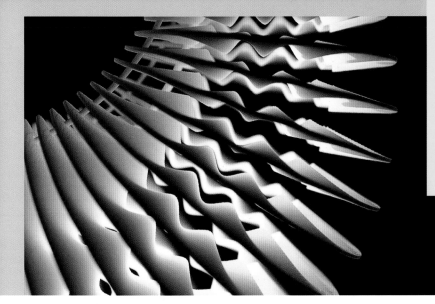

# Operations

A single manufacturing machine is unlikely to produce vast quantities of consumer goods, instead a host of equipment, people and suppliers is usually required to achieve this. The organisation of numerous machines and production processes is a vast subject and this section illustrates some of the key principles of operations and how they impact upon the work of designers.

### Conformance

Conformance is the practice of testing a product to see if it has been made to the correct manufacturing specifications and (in some cases) the correct legal requirements. It can involve a variety of destructive or non-destructive testing methods as well as sampling and statistical theory. It is easy for a designer to think that manufacturing is the problem of the production engineer and for the production engineer to think that finding defects is the responsibility of the testing department. However, a 'quality' approach is for everyone to consider these issues and to work together in avoiding problems before they occur.

### Globalisation

Over the last 40 years, world exports have doubled as the possibility of working, operating and trading beyond the immediate national boundaries grows, spurred on by technical and political developments and the need to compete on a larger scale.

It is argued that this exchange of cultures and products has helped to alleviate war and need. Others argue that globalisation leads to the decline of local cultures and local authority as well as contributing to global environmental damage. Should designers aim to design for a global market and risk the sustainable future of their planet, or should they stay localised at the possible expense of their own livelihood? Many designers are continually looking at ways of trying to achieve the best of both worlds.

### Parametric design

A design and its features might be defined by a number of key parameters, such as its height or weight. If these are linked then it is possible to change an entire design by simply changing one parameter. For example, suppose the depth of a product is required to be half of its height, then changing the height will automatically change the depth.

This principle means considering CAD as a feature-based (rather than a geometric) modeller, and is a very powerful technique. It means libraries of standard feature parts can be used, which saves design time and means that it's possible to make simple changes in solid model CAD drawings without having to start again if a design needs to be changed. It also offers the designer a chance to produce non-standard designs quickly in order to meet a customer's specific requirements, or to generate designs using interesting or mathematical links.

### ▶ Jellyfish House by Iwamoto Scott

The Jellyfish House includes a range of sensors that enables the skin of the house to monitor light, heat and water – even in a contaminated environment – and to react accordingly. The project draws on digital modelling and finite element analysis of a phase-change material to achieve a structure that fluctuates between solid and liquid states.

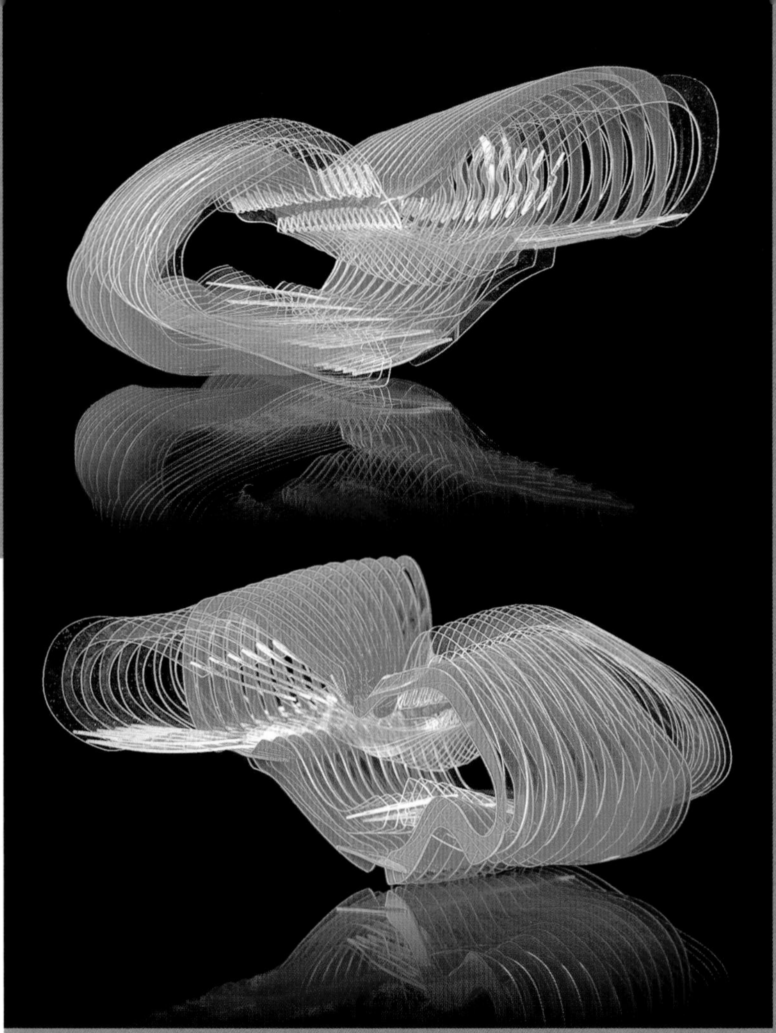

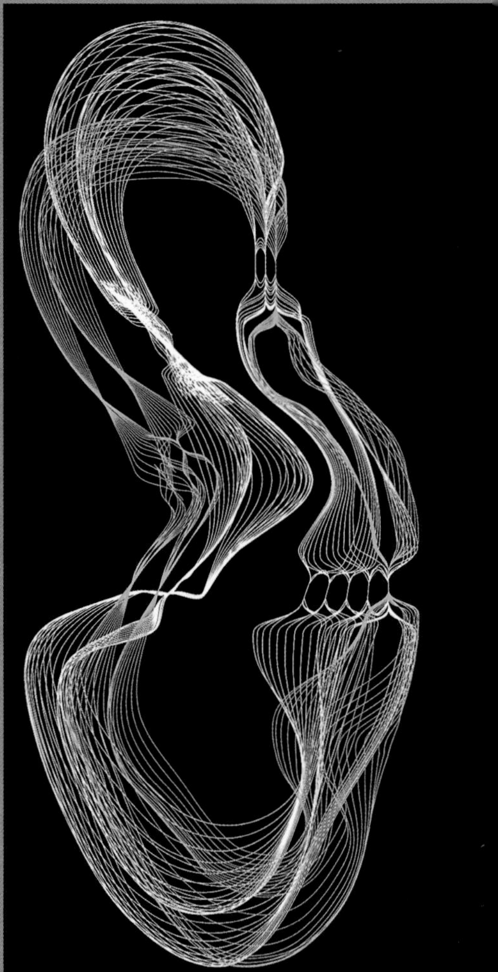





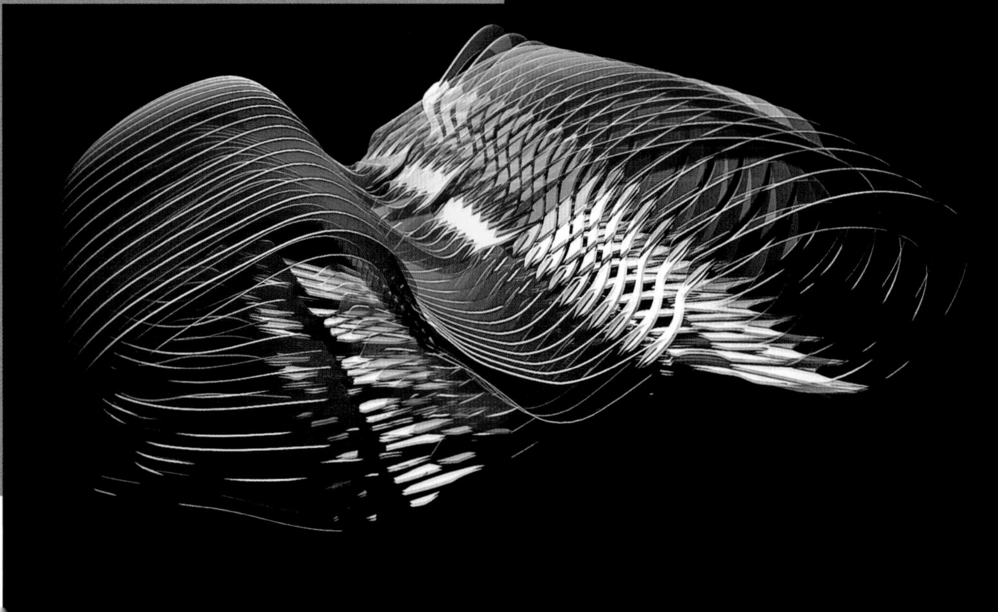

◀ **Achim Menges Morpho Design Experiment No.1**
This is another example of collaborative design linking artists and technologists. This experiment uses digital means to generate complex geometric planes. The curves of these planes are then explored and linked through further analytical software. The programming can be set to develop increasingly complex, morphing shapes yet be bound by the reality of what can actually be manufactured by laser cutting.
Photographs:
Achim Menges

Globalisation has changed us into a company that searches the world, not just to sell or to source, but to find intellectual capital – the world's best talents and greatest ideas.
**Jack Welch, formerly Chairman and Chief Executive Officer, General Electric**

## Modular design

The principle behind modular design is to view a product or a range of products as a system that can be divided into smaller parts. These smaller parts are then designed to a common format (or standardised). For example, a company producing three products 'A', 'B' and 'C', with three different motors, might find it more cost-effective to use the same motor for each different design, even if this means using a larger motor than the product needed. This is because the one motor can be produced in larger numbers using the cheaper techniques of mass production (or obtaining larger supplier discounts).

This principle is often obscured if designers are working in a large organisation and on a single, highly visible product that requires individual production. But imagine the ordering and storage savings that can be made by a company with a wide product range that uses three bolt sizes (say M5, M10 and M15) rather than 300. A designer might initially calculate that they need an M30 bolt in their design, but instead will specify two M15 bolts. In these cases, the issue is how to capture the systems and commonality across the range of products and this requires the designer to be able to access good data management systems. Modularity in design is also a key ingredient in allowing consumers to choose their own combination of features and therefore have more choice in the individual nature of their particular product.

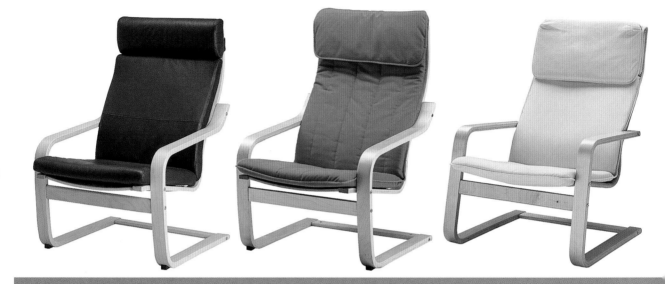

**◄ Chaise Longue No.4 by Tom Raffield**
Raffield's design incorporates local, unseasoned timbers such as oak and ash and uses innovative steam bending techniques to create complex, expressive and challenging products. In this example, the product represents a craft-based approach to design. Only a limited number of the product has been created.

### POÄNG chair by Noburu Nakamura for Ikea

The POÄNG chair is made from bent and glued beechwood veneers that are stained with clear acrylic lacquer, solid beech rails, polypropylene-support fabric and leather seating. It is one of Ikea's top-selling lines and has been purchased by many of the 583 million visitors to the company's stores worldwide.

We shall make electric lighting so cheap that only rich people will be able to afford a candle.
**Thomas Edison**

### Supply chains

In design, it is relatively easy now to fax or email a sketch from one country to another and to have a product made and shipped in just a few days. Behind this simple façade, however, lies a complex network of financial systems, communications technologies, transport operations and trade agreements. The globalisation of designing, sourcing, manufacturing, transporting and trading across the world involves multiple links and networks referred to as supply chains, and the management of these is complex and sophisticated.

Even if designers have elected not to enter the global marketplace, whether they should utilise the global supply chain in order to get the right materials, manufacturing and know-how at the lowest costs needed to deliver their ideal product – knowing that these chains might be contributing towards environmental and sustainable damage – is another issue that designers must consider.

### Just in time

On the face of it, the process of reducing stocks of raw materials and components in a factory and choosing instead to have these items delivered as and when needed (usually 'just in time' or JIT) is a production technique. It does, though, have a profound relationship with design.

As the supply chains become sharper and more efficient at delivering, the production batch sizes can become smaller and smaller. If production is flexible enough (and the design modular and robust) then the batch size can eventually approach a unit size of one. In other words, products can be mass-produced but on a one-by-one basis. If this is linked to sales, then products are effectively individually made to order for each consumer with no storage requirements and no waste.

# Salter Housewares

## Biography

Salter Housewares has been in the weighing business since the 1700s and is a leading player in kitchen scales with around a 40% share of the UK market alone. History can, however, count for little in the commercial world where a failure to innovate can spell disaster. The kitchenware market is a prime example with new products being released on regular basis, not only by traditional competitors, but by new, dynamic companies who are able to enter the market because of the relatively straightforward technology involved.

▶ **Kitchen scales 1007 model by Salter Housewares**

## The Salter 1007 model

The primary function of scales is of course to weigh matter, but the designers at Salter also have to meet several other market needs: the need for compactness in busy kitchens, the need for 'style' in modern lives, the need for cleanliness and hygiene and the need for ease of use.

The 1007 model is designed to meet these needs in a number of ways. It has a very individual ring shape that gives it a distinctive and aesthetic form and the flat, doughnut shape allows the product to be easily stored. The central, circular platform is made of glass, which is hygienic, easily cleaned and resistant to staining. It is also very functional, allowing ordinary dishes to be used as the measuring bowl or for ingredients to be placed straight onto the platform. The digital readout has unusually large bright digits that are shown on a black background, which gives a very clear display. Finally, the scales also have an 'add and weigh' feature that allows ingredients to be added one after the other whilst continually weighing. This saves the need to empty or re-zero each time and supports the way in which cooking through a recipe is actually done.

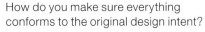

## Q&As

Are you able to design a single
global product?

**Karen Brown (Salter Housewares)**
It makes economic sense to try and design
one product that appeals to as wide a
customer base as possible, but we are
aware of the fact that different markets
have different peculiarities.... The dial
of UK scales [for example], will typically
include older imperial units as well as
metric, whilst a European version will
show metric readings only.... A modular
approach helps to meet those differences.

How do you make sure everything
conforms to the original design intent?

**KB** We use consumer focus groups
regularly to ensure that customer needs
are kept to the forefront of the design.
We also make a point of seeking feedback
from our retailers too, as this can be
extremely informative. With regard
to actual manufacturing conformance,
like most companies we have rigorous
test procedures and work to ISO 9001
(Quality Management Systems).... Good
communications are a key to ensuring
conformity, particularly in ensuring that
we and our suppliers are working to the
same specifications and requirements.

How quickly does it all work?

**KB** Our new product development
process typically takes around six to nine
months from concept to manufacture.
We can reduce this time on occasion if
necessary, but this is the sensible speed....
The whole development process requires
rigid scheduling and attention to detail,
but it's not a purely mechanical process.
We have a good mix of both young and
experienced designers in the team to
ensure that we maintain creativity and
innovation at the same time as producing
practical and manufacturable designs.

# Chapter summary

Some of the issues explored in this chapter, such as costing, production methods and materials and operations are areas that product designers can sometimes find less exciting, certainly in comparison with issues of creativity, technology, function and aesthetics. But this should not be the case. These are the regular, everyday work issues of most designers. It is attention to these details that can make or break a product and that have transformed the industrialised world. A well-made product can transform people's lives, not just physically, but mentally too – and there is a very satisfying feel to generating products that work well and are designed with an elegant use of everyday materials and manufacturing processes.

Some of the most exciting new designs are the result of successful experiments and thinking by talented designers using new ways of working and manufacturing techniques. These are rich areas of exploration and many designers and design movements have made their names by being associated with these pioneering works.

The chapter has also touched on some issues that are raised as a result of the way new products are created. Many designers, for example, are facing up to the challenges of designing more sustainable products. Given the predictions for the future of the planet, this may present us with a new revolution in design.

## Exercise 1

Designers, industrial companies and research organisations seek to find improvements to existing manufacturing techniques. Some of these remain confidential, but others are made explicit through patents or at trade shows and in magazine promotions. Identify and select a recent manufacturing development and apply it either to the design of a new concept product or to the improvement of an existing product.

## Exercise 2

'Ikea is a design-related organisation bringing style to the consumer mass market.' Discuss whether you agree with this statement and contrast it with the ideals of either the Arts and Crafts movement or the Bauhaus movement.

## Exercise 3

Most designers attempt to get a product 'right' first time, but inevitably there are improvements to be made. Select a product of your own choice and redesign it to make it 20 per cent easier to manufacture. You should ensure that you do not change the essence of the product or make changes that are detrimental to its appearance or function. You might look at manufacturing techniques, assembly methods or operational processes.

◀ **Reduced Carbon Footprint Souvenirs by Hector Serrano**

Souvenirs and novelty gifts might be small, but they can have a high carbon footprint, especially if they are made in one country, transported overseas, then stored and redistributed in another country. The digital files for these gifts, however, can be emailed to the recipient and rapid prototyped locally, thus incurring a much lower energy requirement. This concept idea works on the assumption that rapid prototyping technology is becoming ever smaller and cheaper.

Hi Sue,
London is great! We have been lucky enough to experience the British weather! But we have enjoyed ourselves so much! Miss you loads!
Max and Jane 2007

REDUCED CARBON FOOTPRINT SOUVENIR BY HÉCTOR SERRANO

# The marketplace

If money is your hope for independence you will never have it. The only real security that a man will have in this world is a reserve of knowledge, experience, and ability.

**Henry Ford**

**Developing a new product can be a long and strenuous process and it can be infuriating to see competitors simply copying the fruits of this labour and reaping the rewards for a fraction of the effort. It can be equally frustrating to see a well-designed product fail because of poor attention to the selling process. The designer has a role to play in ensuring the success of a product even after it has left the drawing board and the factory gate.**

◀ **Hand wash packaging by Karim Rashid for Method products**

# Preparing to sell

This chapter introduces some of the important issues for designers to consider as manufactured products move towards being sold in the commercial marketplace. The concept of designing fully functional and safe products has been raised in earlier chapters and this section now highlights the penalties for failing to do this effectively. It also explores the notion of accumulated knowledge and the ways in which this can be protected.

## Liability

There is often variety in the way that different countries approach liability for products that don't work or that are dangerous. Some will rely on the market's ability to self-regulate whilst others draw more heavily on the law. In most cases, however, designers will have some form of duty of care towards consumers and may be considered negligent if they do not perform this duty during the design process.

In fact, this duty extends beyond purchasers and may include anybody who is injured by a faulty product. Negligence can be a criminal offence and designers can be held responsible even if they are employed inside a company or are working as a consultant for other people. Negligence is a legal issue that has arisen over time through court actions (common law), but governments also stipulate legal requirements through statutory acts. These tend to put the legal onus alongside the ethical reasoning for designers to make products safe before they are released to the market. Actions to reduce liability and risks include making appropriate design calculations, conducting sufficient experiments and tests and undertaking a systematic risk analysis of the product and its production.

## Knowledge

There is a vast array of expertise that can be generated and accumulated in the design process. For example, throughout the process the designer will have learned what the market needs are, how to make products, how to work new materials or old materials in new ways, how to create functions through clever mechanisms, and how to please people. This knowledge can be of value and traded to other people.

It can be surprising to learn that the global trade in knowledge such as this is actually greater than the global trade in goods. This might mean that your knowledge in how to make a particular product is worth more to you than the income generated by the sales of the product. Knowledge management is about the ability of a designer or organisation to capture and exploit this information. Companies that are good at knowledge management become better and better at generating new products and develop a strategic advantage by becoming associated synonymously with innovation.

## Patents

The legislative protection given to knowledge is termed intellectual property rights (IPR) and these include copyrights, trademarks, database rights, moral rights and patents. The essence of a patent is to protect technical or functional innovations, which might include the way a product works, the way it is made or used, or any new materials or manufacturing techniques employed. The innovations should not be trivial (so they should have commercial value) and must be innovative (so there should be some originality), and all work must be kept confidential.

Some countries award patents to the designer who is 'first to invent' whilst others reward those who are 'first to file' a patent application. The key implication in either case is to not delay in filing for a patent and to keep progress records in authenticated log books. If granted, the patent affords protection against reproduction by others for a period of normally up to 20 years.

## Design rights

Most countries have an IPR that allow a designer to protect the form and shape of their work. These are referred to with terms such as industrial design, design right or registered design. Sometimes these are automatically granted and sometimes they must be applied for. The rules vary and one of the issues around IPRs and the disparity between the legislation in different countries has made it difficult to set up a worldwide form of design protection.

In the UK, design right is an automatic right that protects the form of three-dimensional shapes against copying. More protection is afforded by registering the design (registered design), which protects any aesthetic form, including two-dimensional patterns, against any form of reproduction.

## Commercial protection

Securing intellectual property rights can be a slow and an expensive process, particularly if other parties challenge your applications in the courts. Smaller companies and designers, or those in fast-moving industries, may prefer to use commercial methods to protect their products. This includes concealing technical know-how, ensuring sales through brand loyalty, or introducing new and better products at a faster rate than competitors can respond.

## Information trading

The 'weightless economy' and 'post-Fordism' are two of the many terms that refer to the global trade in information and know-how which acknowledge the move by some countries away from a manufacturing base towards service, knowledge or creatively driven economies.

We'll just have to make it better.
**Joe Colombo
(in response to the plagiarism of his work)**

# Sir James Dyson

## Biography

James Dyson was born in Norfolk, England in 1947 and began his design career at Central St Martins College of Art and Design and the Royal College of Art. His product designs include the Sea Truck (a high-speed watercraft) and the Ballbarrow (a type of wheelbarrow), but he is probably best known for inventing the dual cyclone bagless vacuum cleaner, which works on the principle of cyclonic separation. Together, these products have brought him worldwide recognition, a knighthood and generated a net worth of around £1bn (US$1.6bn).

## ▶ Dyson Cylinder vacuum cleaner

Dyson employs a modular approach to design. Currently, Dyson's range of 13 different cleaning devices is targeted at different market segments, but many share common features including root 'cyclone'™ technology. Like many large organisations, Dyson will ask consumers to register their details as part of their knowledge management programme.

Photograph: Dyson Ltd.

## Patent protection

Dyson is keenly concerned with function in design, resigning at one point from the board of London's Design Museum citing its over-reverence to 'style'. His determination to get things right is well documented in his long struggle (over a five-year period) to get the concept of the dual cyclone vacuum cleaner perfected. This period saw him create over 5,000 prototypes and risk his property and future financial security. What enabled Dyson to take this risk was an inherent belief in the product (which stemmed from his observation of air-conditioning plants combined with his creative link to domestic cleaning) and the security afforded in the form of intellectual property rights.

A patent for the invention allowed Dyson to take his finished prototype to a range of existing vacuum cleaner companies, although none took up the idea and eventually he borrowed £600,000 (US$960,000) to set up his own company, Dyson Appliances. Despite being one of the most expensive vacuum cleaners on the market and with very little in the way of sales promotion (relying instead on word of mouth), the Dyson cleaner was a huge sales success and Dyson's patent protection then proved invaluable when designs similar to his began to appear on the market; Dyson pursued a number of intellectual property court cases.

Hoover denied any infringement of Dyson's intellectual property rights arguing that the technology behind the dual cyclone involved nothing that was not generally known within the industry. The Triple Vortex vacuum cleaner was banned from sale in 2000 after the company was found guilty of patent infringement. The judge considered that the whirlwind principle remained the same and that 'throughout the development of the Vortex cleaner, Hoover was aware of patent claims concerning cyclonic vacuum cleaners, including those claims contained within Dyson patents.' Hoover was ordered to pay damages to Dyson, and forced to launch a new machine that did not infringe the patent. However, Dyson lost the last round of the High Court battle by failing to stop Hoover using the 'Vortex' trademark on its bagless vacuum cleaners.

Dyson has continued to design and manufacture new products, using innovation and intellectual property rights to develop the company further. The company has generated a number of licensing deals for its intellectual property as well as moving its manufacturing base from the UK to the Far East. All of these aspects of modern research, design, manufacture and operation require acute attention to the management of the company's knowledge base.

Hoover's Triple Vortex vacuum cleaner, for example, used centrifugal force and air filters to suck dirt from carpets and furnishings. Hoover avoided using the words 'dual' or 'cyclone' to describe their product, instead referring to 'triple vortex' and 'amplified spin-cleaning' technology, which the company claimed was based on separation technology used to extract sand from oil or gas from crude oil in the North Sea.

### ▶ Dyson vacuum cleaners

The DC24 (this page) and the DC25 (facing page) is a small upright cleaner that sits on top of a ball design, which allows extra manoeuvrability. The cleaner's motor is also housed inside the ball, saving space and lowering the centre of gravity, which again helps the cleaner to be moved easily around tight corners. The ball feature is another innovative development that has helped Dyson to keep ahead of his competitors. Innovation is not, however, restricted to product features and the company offers a range of service-led innovations such as automatic filter change reminders or recycling offers.

Photographs: Dyson Ltd.

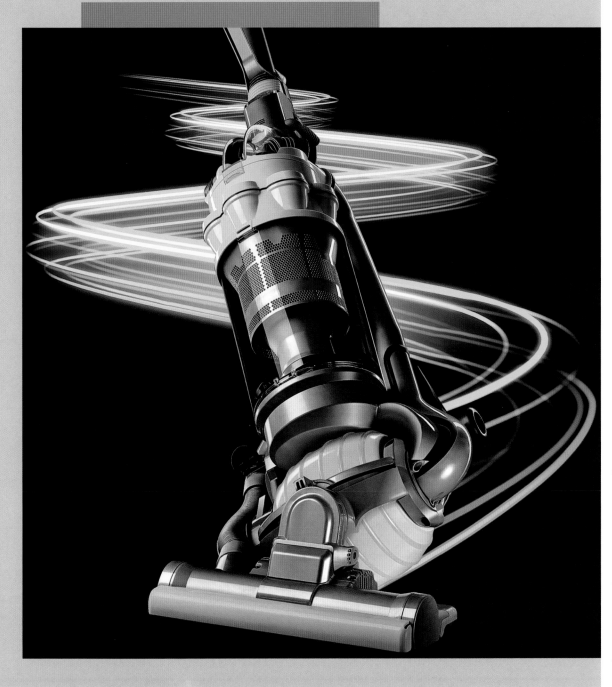

# Marketing

The Industrial Revolution of the late eighteenth and early nineteenth centuries marked the beginning of an era that saw an increasing number of products being made and transported over a wider area, reaching out to a range of new consumers. Marketing developed through a need to provide product information to these new consumers.

As levels of competition have risen, the role of marketing has changed from simply providing information about products to persuading consumers to buy company-specific products. Intense global competition means that persuasion alone is no longer enough and being the first to identify market needs has become crucial. This newer role has often placed marketing at the forefront of determining the strategic direction of a company. This section outlines some of the ways that these marketing functions relate directly to product design.

## Marketing mix

Product, price, place and promotion (the four Ps) are regarded as the marketing tools that can be used in combination to enable a product to be sold in the most effective way. Packaging, for example, has traditionally held a protective and transport role, but in a vastly competitive world the immediate view and appearance of a product can have a profound effect on its sales and can form a vital part of promoting a product – particularly for fast moving consumer goods. A designer has acute insights into the mindset of the market – about what they like, what they might pay and how they behave – and should therefore work closely in creating the optimum product marketing mix.

> The public don't know what they want; it's my job to tell them.
> **Alec Issigonis**

### ▶ Dish soap packaging by Karim Rashid for Method products

Method raised the question as to why many people hide their bathroom products in a cupboard. Packaging design is therefore one strong element of their marketing mix. Karim Rashid's packaging designs include teardrops, truncated cones and a squeeze bottle design that includes an unusual pinch-neck feature. These elements combine to make a more visually interesting and tactile experience for consumers. Rashid has designed a vast array of products and over 2500 have been put into production.

### ◄ Mirra Chair by Herman Miller Inc.

Whilst 'take-back' is not generally a legal requirement for furniture companies, some have adopted the policy as a part of their corporate strategies. The Mirra Chair is the first of Herman Miller's product range to be designed using a life-cycle methodology and has stemmed from the company's commitment to becoming a sustainable business. The chair is designed for longevity; it has a 12-year warranty period and is 96 per cent recyclable without any compromise in performance or style.

### ◄ LEGO® Factory Fan Designed Exclusive, made by Eric Brok

The LEGO® factory allows visitors to LEGO®'s website to design and build products online, which can then be ordered and delivered by mail. Customers can therefore generate any product to suit their own specifications. LEGO® enhances this feature by allowing consumers to demonstrate their products online. It's a form of mass customisation that companies from a range of different industry sectors are beginning to explore.

Photograph:
The LEGO® Group © 2008

Establish contact with the subconscious of the consumer below the word level. They work with visual symbols instead of words … they communicate faster. They are more direct. There is no work, no mental effort.
**Reeves, Reality in Advertising, 1961**

### Take-back

To make a product so durable that it lasts for longer periods might sound like commercial suicide if the company ends up selling fewer products. However, if customers can recognise the improving value of the product then the reputation of the company is enhanced and sales can increase through greater consumer loyalty (as well as from gaining new customers). This 'partnership' mode of business is increasingly driven by the environmental agenda as more consumers recognise the need to create long-lasting products as part of a more sustainable future. It is the polar opposite to the concept of disposable products or those with planned obsolescence.

More enduring products usually require a change in corporate strategic thinking, including, for example, agreements to buy back or repair, products that break in service, and this presents significant design implications. Products need to be robust, yet easy to disassemble and repair with an increased expected lifetime. In some cases, such as in the electronics industry, it is a legal requirement for companies to take back or otherwise deal by other means with a product when it has reached the end of its normally useful working life.

### Mass customisation

Mass customisation is a relatively new concept that describes a consumer's ability to design his or her own unique product using modern technology to enable the process. A consumer might, for example, go online and select the specific features and dimensions they require for their product. A knowledge management system can then generate a CAD model based on a parameterised and modularised product. This design might then be produced using rapid manufacturing techniques and the final product distributed using global supply chains. It is a process that draws together individuality, customisation, rapid prototyping, rapid manufacture, modular design, just-in-time and knowledge management.

### Branding

Branding represents a move in the late twentieth century towards sales that are based less on a product's features and more on its affective attributes, drawing on issues of emotiveness, semantic meanings and values.

Consider the merits, for example, of promoting a vacuum cleaner that has more than twice the suction power of its rivals (feature-based marketing) against a perception that the vacuum cleaner is so powerful it removes dust and dirt to the point where allergies are reduced and (tacitly) that even lifetimes might be extended (emotional or brand-based marketing).

These emotional connections could naturally link to the affirmative features a designer may have included in the design and, where they are enhanced through lifestyle emphasis and imagery, they become extremely powerful selling techniques. Where there is a commonality in the emotiveness of a product range, the brand can become corporate.

There are debates that suggest the power and intrusiveness of brands is not healthy. It is also argued that innovation can decline when the designer's role is simply to produce an emotionally rich, brand-centric product to the detriment of its performance, functions and features.

### Product service systems

A product service system extends the notion of 'partnership' working between the manufacturer and the consumer even further. In this case, the manufacturer removes the product sale completely and instead provides the requisite service that the product would have performed. The most apparent example of this is in photocopying. Office companies may pay for the number of copies they take from a machine that has been rented rather than bought. This is a win-win-win situation. The customer gets what they want, which in this example is reliable, photocopied paperwork, and the manufacturer wins because they secure a continuing income stream through the loan and service agreements. Notably, the environment wins because the onus is on the designer to create a long-lasting and reliable product (because it is the manufacturer and not the company that will have to repair the machine if it breaks). In a product service system, the designer has to consider not just the creation of a robust product, but to understand completely what it is that the customer really needs and how to deliver it.

For me, the concept of design is more than object-oriented; it encompasses the design of processes, systems and institutions as well. Increasingly, we need to think about designing the types of institutions we need to get things done in this rapidly accelerating world.
**John Seely Brown, Chief Scientist, Xerox Corporation**

## ► Nokia 5100 mobile phone

The Nokia 5100 is water- and shock-resistant with a tactile rubberised housing that has a reputation for durability. This makes it appealing to a market sector looking for a rugged product.

Nokia has been described as the world's fifth most valuable brand. It has achieved this with help from a brand philosophy that references the basic human need for social connections and contact.

# Vertu

### Biography

Vertu is a British-based manufacturer and retailer of luxury mobile phones. The company is an independently run, wholly owned subsidiary of the Finnish mobile phone manufacturer Nokia. Established in 1998, Vertu has pioneered the luxury-end mobile phone market by obtaining an upmarket brand profile (in the same way that Rolex has done with the watch market).

Vertu's aims are bold for many reasons. A troubled global economy tends not to favour high-value goods and the company's position stands in direct contrast to the move seen in many industries towards more economical products. Additionally, the Vertu brand is not supported by years of trading, which could bring it the heritage of, say, Rolex or Rolls-Royce. Another factor is that mobile phones represent rapidly moving technology, so the target market must be persuaded to spend a lot of money (typically between 5,000 and 20,000 euros), on a product that performs in much the same way as cheaper models do and which might become dated very quickly. Finally, the market is highly competitive and rivals include not just other phone companies such as Mobiado and GoldVish, but the real possibility that luxury brands such as Louis Vuitton, Prada or Omega may launch mobile phones as part of their own brand extension strategies.

## ◄ Signature by Vertu

Vertu's Signature range incorporates some of the most expensive and exclusive mobile phones in the world. Vertu is a crafts-based manufacturer and the company's attention to materials makes products that can be likened to works of art.

Photograph: Vertu

## The Vertu brand

In facing its corporate challenge, Vertu has the key advantage of pioneering the niche luxury market (whilst its competitors were perhaps focusing solely on technical innovation), but ultimately its long-term success must lie with the abilities of its skilled design team.

The team, headed by principal designer Frank Nuovo, has sought to meet this challenge by using luxury materials such as white gold, platinum and premium leather. Sapphires, the second hardest of the gemstones only to diamond, are used to create scratchproof screens and rubies are used for low friction bearings on many of the product's moving parts. However, designing for this type of brand profile is not just about utilising expensive materials. The team is credited with a particular understanding of how mobile phones 'connect' with people – an empathetic rather than purely technological approach is thus taken.

Included in the design features of a Vertu mobile phone is a patented concierge key that links customers directly to a round-the-clock service team offering lifestyle support, in much the same way as a hotel concierge operates. There is also an understanding in the way that its target consumers appreciate craft rather than mass production. Each telephone is constructed using handmade techniques and in the case of Vertu's Signature range, this incorporates 288 components and 96 quality control inspections. This time-consuming but artisan approach represents a move towards custom-made and crafted products. To further enhance design and the functional attributes of exclusivity and individuality, Vertu's products are sold only through specialised or high-end stores such as Harrods (London) and Barneys (New York).

Despite the successes achieved so far, there are ongoing challenges and decisions for the Vertu designers to address. Should the products be made modular, allowing technological upgrades to be easily made but at the expense of the company's custom-made philosophy? Should the company continue to use its technology? The design team has already predicted that mobile phones of the future may morph more towards wearable products (in a similar way to watches or jewellery); but how and in what form should this be? Issues such as these serve to demonstrate that design has a much wider role to play (in corporate strategy and branding) than pure product function. The challenge for Vertu's designers is ultimately to understand their customers, bring the product to life and finally deliver the corporate brand strategy.

# Chapter summary

This chapter has set out to explore some of the post-production issues that surround new products and look at why these issues need to be considered by designers at an early stage in the design process. When products get to market they need to work and there can be severe penalties if they do not. A designer must therefore work systematically to ensure that they have considered all possible risks involved and reduced these to the minimum level required to make a product safe.

A great deal of knowledge is generated from the very outset of the design process. For individuals this might simply be expertise retained in their own thoughts, captured through reflection and experience and practised through artisan design. For larger organisations capturing this information might require sophisticated knowledge management systems to ensure that it is retained, valued, disseminated and utilised across the whole company.

Once knowledge is released in the form of a new product, it is relatively easy for others to gain from your hard work and efforts. Intellectual property rights (IPR) protect different aspects of a design. It's important to remember that an idea by itself is rarely capable of being protected and it needs translating into features and designs. It's equally important in doing this not to infringe the IPRs of others by undertaking due diligence. Sometimes IPR is not the appropriate form of protection, but where commercial routes to protect designs are taken these often need the backing of an appropriate corporate strategy. Designers may need to be thinking of the next version as they work on the current version in order to stay ahead of competitors.

The final section has looked at the role of marketing and branding in creating commercial success. The selling of products through the power of emotion might take the product back to the same core values that the designer explored at the very outset of his or her project. The use of mass customisation, take-back and product service systems provide illustrations to some of the newer production and marketing techniques, which may affect the way all products are designed in future.

### Exercise 1

A chainsaw is a highly hazardous product that is capable of causing life-threatening injuries. According to the US Consumer Products Safety Commission there were over 28,500 chain saw injuries in 1999. Yet this product can be purchased in most gardening and do-it-yourself stores. Conduct a risk assessment on a product of your own choosing and incorporate design features that reduce the chances of user injury.

### Exercise 2

Select a product at random. Define the purpose of the product and consider how you might lease the service that this product provides. What are the implications for this in drawing up a design specification?

## ▶ Vasarely Wall Lamp by Janne Kyttänen

This lamp pays homage to Victor Vasarely, considered by many to be the father of optical art. The lamp bulges at its centre, creating a three-dimensional feel and creating unusual patterns and rhythms of light and shadow.

The lamp is made from laser-sintering P2200, which is a fine power that is similar to Polyamide 12 but has higher crystallinity, a higher melting point and anti-oxidation stabilisers.

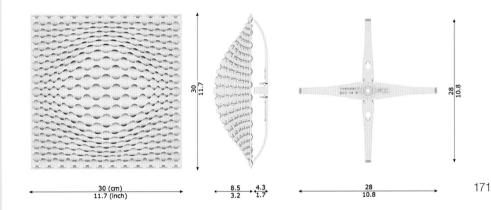

30 (cm)
11.7 (inch)

30
11.7

8.5
3.2

4.3
1.7

28
10.8

28
10.8

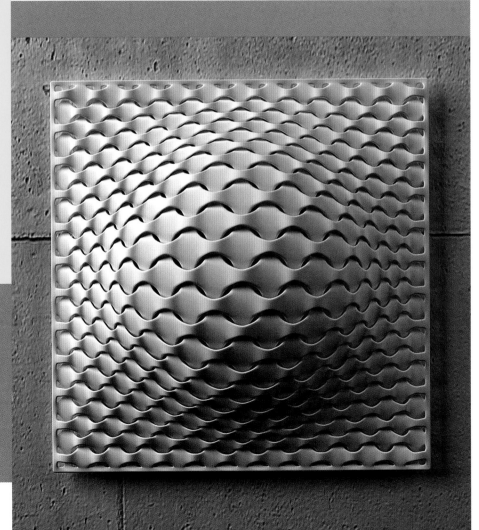

# Conclusion

It can be a surprise to some to learn that design can be as much about philosophy and personal perspective as it can be about determining the right size bolt to use. Sometimes these philosophical debates about where design sits are polemic with fierce advocates on one side or the other, but more often the issues are cloudy. Seeing through the mist can be an important part of a designer's life and through this clarity and their design work they can have an influence on world affairs.

Taking a perspective and being able to look into the future are just two of the many core skills that this book has highlighted as being important to designers. Others have included being imaginative and creative, being analytical and logical, capable of research and problem-solving, being observant, empathetic, knowledgeable, communicative and so on. The list might seem endless. It would be rare, however, to find a designer who is brilliant at all of these things, or indeed one who needs to be brilliant at all of these things.

Different designers may have particular strengths in different areas and this may be down to genes, training or the type of occupation, and the demands of an individual craftsman may be very different to a designer of components in a large multinational company. However, this variety does mean that designers might always be drawing on the experiences and lessons they have learnt in life in more ways perhaps than any other profession. It also means that they can always learn more, improving areas of strength and developing areas of weakness. For those with an opinion, a thirst to face challenges, and a desire to learn and develop, then there can be no better profession to choose than that of product design.

▶ **Furniture by Straight Line Designs**
Probably the only thing common to Straight Line Design's products is that there are few straight lines! Work leans towards the unusual and whimsical with a heavy emphasis on crafted individual consumer requirements.

# Further resources

Resources for design are as wide ranging as the subject area itself, but you might try some of the following examples as places to obtain further information or just as sources of inspiration.

## Journals

Blueprint
Design
Design Week
Domus
ICON
Innovation
International Journal of Design
New Design
Science
Technovation

## Websites

http://www.design4design.com
http://www.designandfun.com
http://www.designmuseum.org
http://www.experimentaldesign.com
http://www.howstuffworks.com
http://www.ulrich-eppinger.net

## Places to visit

Design Museum
Butlers Wharf, 28 Shad Street
London, UK

Victoria & Albert Museum
Kensington, London, UK

Cooper-Hewitt
National Design Museum
Smithsonian Institution, USA

Red Dot Design Museum
Essen, Germany

Vitra Design Museum
Weil am Rhein, Germany

International Design Centre
Nagoya, Japan

Exploratorium
San Francisco, USA

## Exhibitions

100% Design (London)
Designers Block (Global locations)
Milan Furniture Fair (Italy)
International Furnishing show (Cologne, Germany)
London Design Festival

## Competitions and awards

Audi Foundation
British Design & Art Direction Student Awards
Carbonate
Design Week Consumer Product of the year
Corus and Blueprint magazine
Design and Decoration
DesignSense Award
European Design Competition
Eurobest

## Further help

Arts Council England
www.artscouncil.org.uk

Design Association
www.design-association.org

Design Council
www.designcouncil.org.uk

Design Nation
www.designnation.co.uk

Design Research Society
www.designresearchsociety.org

European Academy of Design
www.europeanacademyofdesign.org

European Institute of Innovation and Technology
ec.europa.eu/eit

Royal Society for the Encouragement
of Arts, Manufacture and Commerce (RSA)
www.rsa.org.uk

Society of Designer Craftsmen
www.societyofdesignercraftsmen.org.uk

# Acknowledgements

This book would not have been possible without the efforts and support of Leonie Taylor. Many thanks for your picture researching endeavours. Similarly I would like to thank David Shaw for the book's page and cover design.

Also with grateful thanks to all those designers and organisations that willingly contributed and allowed us to reproduce their work on these pages and supplied detailed information about the designs.

A final thank you to Caroline Walmsley, Brian Morris, Helen Stone and all at AVA Publishing who have supported the project throughout.

175

Lynne Elvins/Naomi Goulder

Working with ethics
The Fundamentals
of Product Design

178

The subject of ethics is not new, yet its consideration within the applied visual arts is perhaps not as prevalent as it might be. Our aim here is to help a new generation of students, educators and practitioners find a methodology for structuring their thoughts and reflections in this vital area.

AVA Publishing hopes that these **Working with ethics** pages provide a platform for consideration and a flexible method for incorporating ethical concerns in the work of educators, students and professionals. Our approach consists of four parts:

The **introduction** is intended to be an accessible snapshot of the ethical landscape, both in terms of historical development and current dominant themes.

The **framework** positions ethical consideration into four areas and poses questions about the practical implications that might occur. Marking your response to each of these questions on the scale shown will allow your reactions to be further explored by comparison.

The **case study** sets out a real project and then poses some ethical questions for further consideration. This is a focus point for a debate rather than a critical analysis so there are no predetermined right or wrong answers.

A selection of **further reading** for you to consider areas of particular interest in more detail.

Ethics is a complex subject that interlaces the idea of responsibilities to society with a wide range of considerations relevant to the character and happiness of the individual. It concerns virtues of compassion, loyalty and strength, but also of confidence, imagination, humour and optimism. As introduced in ancient Greek philosophy, the fundamental ethical question is *what should I do?* How we might pursue a 'good' life not only raises moral concerns about the effects of our actions on others, but also personal concerns about our own integrity.

In modern times the most important and controversial questions in ethics have been the moral ones. With growing populations and improvements in mobility and communications, it is not surprising that considerations about how to structure our lives together on the planet should come to the forefront. For visual artists and communicators it should be no surprise that these considerations will enter into the creative process.

Some ethical considerations are already enshrined in government laws and regulations or in professional codes of conduct. For example, plagiarism and breaches of confidentiality can be punishable offences. Legislation in various nations makes it unlawful to exclude people with disabilities from accessing information or spaces. The trade of ivory as a material has been banned in many countries. In these cases, a clear line has been drawn under what is unacceptable. But most ethical matters remain open to debate, among experts and lay-people alike, and in the end we have to make our own choices on the basis of our own guiding principles or values. Is it more ethical to work for a charity than for a commercial company? Is it unethical to create something that others find ugly or offensive?

Specific questions such as these may lead to other questions that are more abstract. For example, is it only effects on humans (and what they care about) that are important, or might effects on the natural world require attention too? Is promoting ethical consequences justified even when it requires ethical sacrifices along the way? Must there be a single unifying theory of ethics (such as the Utilitarian thesis that the right course of action is always the one that leads to the greatest happiness of the greatest number), or might there always be many different ethical values that pull a person in various directions?

As we enter into ethical debate and engage with these dilemmas on a personal and professional level, we may change our views or change our view of others. The real test though is whether, as we reflect on these matters, we change the way we act as well as the way we think. Socrates, the 'father' of philosophy, proposed that people will naturally do 'good' if they know what is right. But this point might only lead us to yet another question: *how do we know what is right?*

**You**

### What are your ethical beliefs?

Central to everything you do will be your attitude to people and issues around you. For some people their ethics are an active part of the decisions they make everyday as a consumer, a voter or a working professional. Others may think about ethics very little and yet this does not automatically make them unethical. Personal beliefs, lifestyle, politics, nationality, religion, gender, class or education can all influence your ethical viewpoint.

Using the scale, where would you place yourself? What do you take into account to make your decision? Compare results with your friends or colleagues.

**Your client**

### What are your terms?

Working relationships are central to whether ethics can be embedded into a project and your conduct on a day-to-day basis is a demonstration of your professional ethics. The decision with the biggest impact is whom you choose to work with in the first place. Cigarette companies or arms traders are often-cited examples when talking about where a line might be drawn, but rarely are real situations so extreme. At what point might you turn down a project on ethical grounds and how much does the reality of having to earn a living effect your ability to choose?

Using the scale, where would you place a project? How does this compare to your personal ethical level?

01  02  03  04  05  06  07  08  09  10

01  02  03  04  05  06  07  08  09  10

## Your specifications

### What are the impacts of your materials?

In relatively recent times we are learning that many natural materials are in short supply. At the same time we are increasingly aware that some man-made materials can have harmful, long-term effects on people or the planet. How much do you know about the materials that you use? Do you know where they come from, how far they travel and under what conditions they are obtained? When your creation is no longer needed, will it be easy and safe to recycle? Will it disappear without a trace? Are these considerations the responsibility of you or are they out of your hands?

Using the scale, mark how ethical your material choices are.

## Your creation

### What is the purpose of your work?

Between you, your colleagues and an agreed brief, what will your creation achieve? What purpose will it have in society and will it make a positive contribution? Should your work result in more than commercial success or industry awards? Might your creation help save lives, educate, protect or inspire? Form and function are two established aspects of judging a creation, but there is little consensus on the obligations of visual artists and communicators toward society, or the role they might have in solving social or environmental problems. If you want recognition for being the creator, how responsible are you for what you create and where might that responsibility end?

Using the scale, mark how ethical the purpose of your work is.

01 02 03 04 05 06 07 08 09 10

01 02 03 04 05 06 07 08 09 10

One aspect of product design that raises an ethical dilemma is the environmental impact that materials can have. This issue needs more consideration, particularly if an object is knowingly designed to become waste after only a short time. The advent of synthetic plastics in the early twentieth century opened the door to mass production of cheap, attractive goods that democratised the ownership of consumer products.

Planned obsolescence became a lucrative strategy for large companies in the 1950s and this fuelled ongoing product replacements through styling changes. But as the longer-term impacts of manmade plastics became more widely understood in the second half of the 20th century, it has become clear that there is an environmental price to pay for human convenience and consumer choice. How much responsibility should a product designer have in this situation? If designers wish to minimise the environmental impacts of products, what might they most usefully do?

Newspaper editor László Bíró (1899–1985), found that he wasted a great deal of time filling his pen with ink, cleaning up smudges and tearing pages with the nib of his fountain pen. With help from his brother, Bíró began to work on a new type of pen and fitted a tiny ball in its tip that was free to turn in a socket. He filed a British patent for the design in June 1938.

In 1945, Marcel Bich, along with his partner Edouard Buffard, bought a factory in France and went into business as the maker of parts for fountain pens and mechanical lead pencils. As his business began to grow, the development of the ballpoint pen was advancing in both Europe and the US. Bich saw the great potential for this new writing instrument and obtained the patent rights from Bíró to manufacture his own. In 1950, Bich launched his new reliable pen at an affordable price. He called it BIC (the 'h' from Bich was dropped in order to avoid the English pronunciation *bitch*).

The BIC biro was a mass-produced consumer item that was cheap enough that if it were accidentally lost, the owner would be unlikely to care. Its mass success comes out of the BIC product philosophy: 'just what is necessary', a phrase driven by simplicity, functionality, quality and price. The aim is for harmony between the form of a product and the use it is designed for.

182

A BIC pen can draw a line up to three kilometres long. It is made from polystyrene (transparent barrel), polypropylene (cap), tungsten carbide (ball) and brass/nickel silver (tip). The environmental impact of a BIC biro comes predominantly from the materials, with approximately five grams of oil-based plastic used in the manufacture of each pen. Because of their widespread use by schoolchildren, all ballpoint ink formulas are non-toxic and the manufacturing and content of ink is regulated in most countries.

The relatively recent addition of the vent hole in the cap of the BIC pen was designed to minimise the risk of choking should it be swallowed. This is a requirement to comply with international safety standards after an incident in the late 1980s where a young child in the UK died due to the inhalation of a pen cap. Nine similar deaths had been recorded in the previous fifteen years, none have been recorded in the UK since the publication of this safety standard.

The BIC biro has become an industrial design classic. In 2002 it entered the permanent collections of the Museum of Modern Art (MOMA) in New York. In September 2005, BIC sold its one hundred billionth disposable ballpoint, making it the world's best-selling pen.

**Should designers, producers or users have responsibility if a product causes injury?**
**Is it unethical to design a product to be thrown away?**
**Would you have worked on this project?**

Our definitions of positive impact have become too narrow as designers. Focused perhaps too often on pleasing our own ego.
**Tim Brown (CEO of IDEO)**
From a transcription of a presentation given at the InterSections conference in 2007

AIGA
*Design business and ethics*
2007, AIGA

Eaton, Marcia Muelder
*Aesthetics and the good life*
1989, Associated University Press

Ellison, David
*Ethics and aesthetics in European modernist literature*
2001, Cambridge University Press

Fenner, David EW (Ed.)
*Ethics and the arts: an anthology*
1995, Garland Reference Library of Social Science

Gini, Al (Ed.)
*Case studies in business ethics*
2005, Prentice Hall

McDonough, William and Braungart, Michael
'Cradle to Cradle: Remaking the Way We Make Things'
2002

Papanek, Victor
'Design for the Real World: Making to Measure'
1971

United Nations
Global Compact the Ten Principles
www.unglobalcompact.org/AboutTheGC/TheTenPrinciples/index.html

Working with ethics